The Definitive Guide to Hunting, Gathering, and Flaunting Superior Vintage Wares

Sheila Zubrod & David Stern

 HarperPerennial

A Division of HarperCollins*Publishers*

HarperCollins books may be purchased for educational, business, or sales promotional use. For information please write: Special Markets Department, HarperCollins Publishers, Inc., 10 East 53rd Street, New York, NY 10022.

FIRST EDITION

Designed by Amy Hershman and David Stern
Illustrations by Martin Ledyard

Library of Congress Cataloging-in-Publication Data

Zubrod, Sheila.
    Flea : the definitive guide to hunting, gathering, and flaunting
    superior vintage wares / Sheila Zubrod and David Stern. — 1st ed.
        p.   cm.
    ISBN 0-06-092771-2
    1. Flea markets.   I. Stern, David, 1964–   .   II. Title.
    HF5482.15.Z83   1997
    381'.192—dc21   97-6424

97 98 99 00 01 ❖/RRD 10 9 8 7 6 5 4 3 2 1

For our mothers, Ceil Zubrod and Jennifer Stern

CONTENTS

ACKNOWLEDGMENTS

On Behalf of Flea

A number of people made *Flea* possible. In particular we are indebted to Lisa Bankoff and Eric Steel for putting us on the road, to Amy Hershman for giving *Flea* visual shape and bite, and Beth Bortz for driving us to the finish line.

Sheila would also like to thank her rat pack: Kelly Gordon, Cheryl Brantner, Bill Butler, Christine Bastoni, David Landay, Kerry MacBride, and Valerie Gelb for their constructive criticism and their wildly unstinting encouragement.

David would also like to thank his wife, Zane, who always manages to find something we really really "need" at every flea market outing. In addition: Richard Feldman at ICM and Andrew Steinberg for believing in our ideas, Donald Miller, Tommy Steele, Cheryl Meyer, and everyone at Maddocks & Company.

We are also grateful to Ellen Breslow, Jeffrey Barnes, Elizabeth Guildersleeve, Marilyn Bauer, Edward Cabot, Andrew Cullinan, Robin Gaines, Lois Grange, Anne Groer, David Spriggs, Davy Jones, Barry Shulman, Allan Moss, Jim Oliveira, Jon Handelsman, Erica Meyer, Richard Mauro, Richard Merkin, Thomas Oatman, Caralina Gramm Bundt, and Norio Saito for generously sharing their insights, their abundant knowledge, and their mind's eye.

And to the many enthusiasts who said they would be the first in line to buy this book, we thank you for the encouragement we far too frequently needed to complete our mission.

The opening poem, "Green Glass Beads," is my homage to Harold Monroe's poem "Overheard on a Salt Marsh" written in 1928. He had a style that not only blew me away in third grade but shaped my relationship to the world around me.

—Sheila Zubrod

SHOPPING
for the 21st
Century

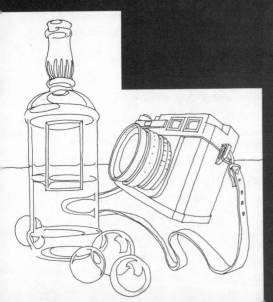

Green glass beads
I love you so,
I shall howl at
the moon
till you're mine.

CHAPTER 1

There is something in the air at a flea market.
Something that is weirdly, emotionally satisfying in a modern sort of way. Maybe it's a molecular dance, produced by
the nutty combinations of all those things from different
decades, lying side by side. Where else—outside of a gallery
at the height of Surrealism—would a rusted piece of farm
machinery sit next to a handmade rocket ship, which sits
next to a Lucite salad bowl, which sits next to an Arts and
Crafts pot, and so on?

In fact, if you're accustomed only to the carefully presented,
sanitized, macro-vision retail environments of the 1990s, the
sheer, random messiness of a flea market is invariably a brac-
ing, cold-water shock. However, it does prepare you for the
work ahead—to establish order and make connections.
Because at any epic flea market it's up to us, the buyers, to
connect the dots. It's the ultimate hide and seek.

But whatever it is that lures us in, it is wildly contagious. Every weekend millions and millions of Americans flock to these transient Brigadoon-like cities to browse the entire twentieth century, and even some of the nineteenth century. They come to exercise their wits, their eye, and to turn the sport of pricing from spectator to participatory.

Origins of Flea Style

Theory one It's not easy to live in the age of the chip.

It only takes a brief surge of electricity to disable just about anything that's new, such as your phone, your computer, or your television.

Life controlled by unstable software and auxiliary sources is just too complex to be reliable. No one needs to understand the details of how an electronic pulse plays out electronically in order to understand it intuitively. Old stuff can be fixed. New stuff can't.

And worse yet, unlike old Leica cameras that clicked on and on through foxholes and jungles and wind-up watches that never needed batteries, new stuff is rarely known for setting endurance records.

That being the case, you can understand why many people are choosing to make their lives simpler and more reliable by surrounding themselves with simple stuff from a simpler time.

The urge that pulls "junkers" to dusty fields and even dustier sheds across the country could also be primal. It could even be the same itch that motivated medieval crusaders long ago. They too probably left home just to get out of the socio-economic rut they were in with little sense of what they might bring home for the mantelpiece. Some went to search for the grail. Some went for sheer adventure.

The ethos remains the same. At the end of the day, what you buy is curiously irrelevant to the hunt. Even when you've had a bad day in terms of finding an intangibly wonderful thing, you can still return with powerful visual memories to savor: like the austere Yankee architecture that pervades the upstate New York town of Hudson, or the fabled 450-Mile Flea Market that stretches from Covington, Kentucky, to Chattanooga, Tennessee. Yes, you might find a small silver flute along your route—but the stop to commemorate your coup at a local root beer stand will be a part of what you remember as long as that silver flute sits on your mantelpiece. And what's behind the flute is another story entirely . . .

Origins of Flea Style
Theory two The clock is ticking.

Many successful dealers swear our tastes run thirty years backward, i.e., as you're wandering around a flea market these days, the late 1960s should be singing a siren song.
Look for enameled cast-iron cookware, abstract art, even plastic fantastic chairs.

However, other dealers claim the noise you hear is coming from a far bigger clock—the antique *process* itself. By 2001 *all* that stuff gathering dust will be worth more. Not just economically but sentimentally, as a way of making sense of our journey through time. As the countdown to the millennium picks up speed, even the recent twentieth century will suddenly be as far from us as the nineteenth century used to be. This automatically increases the worth of stuff from the '50s, '60s, '70s, *and* '80s, allowing us to think of the *entire* twentieth century as a mall of unlimited possibilities filled with souvenirs par excellence.

So, Arts and Crafts pottery is back. Vintage toasters keep on plugging. Even the old vinyl Scotch Plaid picnic coolers—which the manufacturer used to swear were used by more hospitals to carry body parts than any other cooler—are heading off to the beach one more time.

Every vintage object has a past behind it. Because unlike people—or even institutions—*things* survive. Every history-studded object we bring home enriches our sense of place. Now that we live in apartments, suburban townhouses, and new condominiums—and not old houses layered over time—we need that sense of continuity more than ever. Developments have replaced neighborhoods. Malls have replaced shops. And if all the cosmic dearth that that implies isn't enough, the very furniture and objects we come home to were created by megalithic retail chains like Ikea, Pottery Barn, and Crate & Barrel.

Thanks to a labyrinth of designers, stylists, and researchers, each of these behemoths churns out countless identical objects. Their artisans pore over old books, frequent junk stores, attend antique boutiques, and even travel to international flea markets. Yet no matter how good—or even how striking—the products and furniture they create may look, the real issue is that someone else has done all the work. Each reproduction of a foreign candlestick is a living reminder that some stylist had a great adventure—and we didn't.

Most of us feel that loss acutely. We crave our own authenticity, individuality, and self-expression. And, faced with the repression of our own creative instincts, we revolt. We revolt against all the prefabbed, predigested, prepackaged goods that surround us and suggest that we can't be trusted to pick and choose, coordinate, or get it right. The underground is fighting back.

Our revolt is the alter-economy.

The alter-economy is born of flea markets, green markets, yard sales, stoop sales, auctions, estate sales, junk stores, pawn shops, special event pier shows, antique malls, and Website collectors. Its grass roots have grown and spread like weeds on a bender at the same time that the rest of the world has entrenched itself further and further into catalogs and malls (to the point where the Tokyo airport recently had to build an extension for an extra customs area just to process L.L. Bean packages).

Origins of Flea Style
Theory three Money talks.

There are no more laws of economics left, particularly now that real estate is no longer the big kahuna of all investments. It's a Twilight Zone out there.

Added to layoffs, downsizing, and going-nowhere-fast entry-level jobs, the fine print details of saving money are more important than ever. Spending less has become a necessity *and* an art form. For many people the art of locating well-made stuff they can actually use—at pay-less prices—has become a mission as well as an adventure. It's the best way to get what you pay for.

Flea dealers swear buying vintage furniture is like buying a used car versus a new car. Drive a new car off the lot and you lower its bluebook value faster than a speeding bullet, whereas the value of a used car remains consistent. Similarly, when you buy old furniture—or even used furniture—you're buying a piece at its true value.

Therefore, anytime you can pick from the past *and* pay less, go for it.

In the alter-economy, every weekend brings new, ever-evolving opportunities to hunt down serendipitous stuff in all kinds of local and out-of-the-way markets, from legendary seasonal markets like Brimfield to the well over 3,000 flea markets that now exist in the United States alone. While these flea markets are only the tip of the alter-economy, when you stumble on a great one you'll know why they are at the dead center of its fiery core.

Each one is an economy of its own, where the strength of sheer desire jeopardizes any pretense of objectivity.

No one producing flea markets is making Bill Gates–style money. This scene is not as much about cash as it is about cache. Yet its repercussions both in shaping a new aesthetic and in helping us reclaim our individuality are vivid, powerful, and contagious.

The aesthetic spawned by the burgeoning spread of the alter-economy is based on the uncanny juxtapositions that occur automatically at a flea market. It's the essence of popular culture. Seeing an object stripped of any context is curiously liberating. Things take on a whole new life. In fact, the visual lure of anachronisms has become so popular, you'd be hard pressed these days to pick up any decorating magazine in the world and not find disparate vintage objects prominently featured in every modern layout. The look reflects the kind of style that money alone can't buy. It's about time, chance, and above all an eye for what's personally meaningful.

Origins of Flea Style
Theory four We are what we remember.

Every great market is a 3-D memory lane, with emotional surprises you won't find at a department store. Even if you were raised by wolves, you will invariably find at least one obscure object at a flea market that you had almost forgotten about. This makes the full millennium quotient of twentieth-century flea artifacts satisfying to all age groups.

The re-creation of time can happen in a glance. Unattached bits from the lives of others are begging for psychic recycling, and the object you need to promote a change in your life's situation could be laying on a table in front of you.

Nothing is predictable when you're surrounded by the outpourings of so many lives, especially if a few thousand dealers are bombarding you with unexpected stuff and bizarre combinations. (This may be why the English call flea markets "jumbles.") You'll traipse through market aisles that conjure up surprisingly personal, even intimate, memories and emotions.

In fact, to walk through a flea market is to reconstruct a mosaic of who you've been in this life. In other words, we are what we buy.

Finding your own aesthetic takes work. Before you can put your acquisitions together in ways that reflect your inner vision of peace, harmony, and home, you have to find them, and then imagine them leading a whole new life.

The search can take you far and wide. Who knows on which table or what dusty shelf that obscure object of your desire is waiting? Is it that cluster of Oddfellow ceremonial spears at a yard sale on the side of a road? Or that fifty-year-old doctor's metal instrument cabinet in your uncle's basement? Or that magical Chinese scroll waiting in a Hong Kong flea market?

Origins of Flea Style

Theory five Uplifting art has unusual powers.

In the nineteenth century art equaled religion. That's why museums were open on Sunday. Art was good for the soul.

Art, however, has always reflected the issues of the larger culture. And these days, the chasm between art, design, and salvation has widened. Some say it is increasingly conceptual, embedded in issues of censorship, socio-economic change, and cultural wars.

But no matter what the content, as art becomes increasingly intellectual it drifts further and further away from the emotional experience many still seek.

The new appreciation of "modern antiques" may simply reflect a search for the aesthetic, visual gratification we used to get from contemplating art.

Flea market junkets could be our way of finding some level of truth by tracking the value of visible objects. "Junking" could be our way of searching for what the Japanese call *wabi,* the serenity that comes from viewing an object with lines that are intrinsically, innately, and aesthetically harmonious based on objective criteria.

Or to put it another way, the role of art is to reflect reality. Which means that art changes as the culture changes. Yet these days some of us will invariably feel more fulfilled by an Eva Zeisel–designed Red Wing pot or even a weathered glass float ball than a painted treatise on family values at the Whitney Biennial.

The euphoria of a find ensures that flea markets deliver the kind of authenticity and emotional gratification department stores can't. But peak moments are only half the appeal. The human face of flea markets is built on a principle of interaction that far outstrips the reach of any technological invention.

Built into every single venue of the alter-economy is an unusual element of humanity. Because, unlike other retail experiences, the alter-economy is based on the reality that we often buy the wrong things, or simply buy too much. It lets us simplify our lives by getting rid of extra possessions because the alter-economy is as much about selling as it is about buying.

Origins of Flea Style
Theory six You see what you want to see.

The grail is always changing shape. As our perception of reality changes, so does our perception of art. This is where the Chinese concept of *wu* enters.

Wu describes what you bring to the party—spiritually. It's not about criteria. It's more like rediscovering early Bob Dylan insights. You can find beauty in ugliness or vice versa. It's all in *your* eye. If a mid-century vintage life preserver from a long-gone yacht looks like a work of art to you—well, that's *wu*.

Flea markets are a visual anthem: a testament to the winnowing of wheat from chaff. They're a constantly evolving, shifting dance of people unloading their collections and changing their taste, whether they're in the process of leaving behind their love of American art pottery from the Arts and Crafts decade and moving on to orange plastic-exteriored transistor radios made in Japan—or simply selling off all their cold weather coziness to move down South. It's this particular tango that fuels the alter-economy and gives flea markets a pace and grace all their own. And it's our chance to recover from an adrenaline-charged life . . . and maybe win a souvenir from a favorite decade should the goddess of the hunt be with us.

Origins of Flea Style
Theory seven Flea markets feel good.

Surrealist artists were said to have believed in the soothing qualities of two activities: (1) taking a walk and (2) going to a flea market.

Obviously, both of their early forms of Prozac involved fresh air and a fresh perspective. Even more curiously, both of these cheap vacations somehow led to the creation of fur-lined teacups and architectural tools with no function.

And so it might be logically surmised that flea markets liberate the mind's eye.

The healthful effects of walking are just now being fully documented. Flea markets may be next.

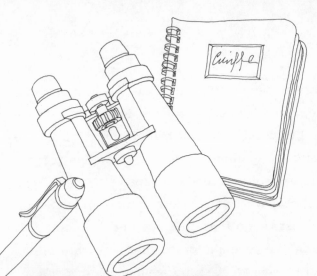

finding
things

CHAPTER

Some people attend flea markets looking for more than adventure or sheer whimsy. They go in search of objects they hope will become enormously more valuable.

One well-known collecting guru urges his readers to actively seek out stuff based on its potential value down the road. Whether it's something those readers might ever *use* or not is not relevant to his idea of collecting as an investment strategy.

His theory works like this: buy old or new merchandise, like Barbie dolls, GI Joes, or Olympic memorabilia—keep the loot in mint condition in the original boxes—and you'll be able to retire in genteel poverty thanks to your profits.

Don't count on it.

Trends aren't easy to predict, especially if everyone else is stockpiling Barbies in their safe deposit boxes as well.

Certainly, some dolls might soar in value, but most will not. There is also a very real possibility that on the exact same day the price of your 1950 Patty Playpal climbs, the price of your 1960 Vinyl Chrissie will take a nosedive. In short, if you're buying to invest, never discount the element of risk in collectibles.

Examples of this yo-yo phenomena don't even have to be financial. On the very day you decide to unload your collection of Bakelite bracelets, you could see someone wearing an armful of translucent amber Bakelite bangles mixed in with silver bracelets—and suddenly Bakelite looks magical again.

So why bother trying to keep up? Why not bring home only those objects that move you for completely personal, even inexplicable reasons? Collect stuff *you* can actually use and enjoy now. These are the true classics. You're better off creating your own collecting guidelines than buying for possible worth somewhere down the road. Face it, anytime hordes of people collect any object, it's over. Things that actually do end up becoming valuable are invariably what no one else gives a damn about—except someone who collected them out of love.

Follow your own deepest instincts. Buy something you can afford for the sheer kick of it—just because it catches your imagination. Let the kite go. It could turn out to be a back issue of pornographic *Bust Out* magazine, a faded, pastel colored pair of miniature Chinoiserie boys and girls made to carry toothpicks in their rickshaws, or feathers from the rain forest. You won't know what you really want until you see it.

The things that will move you can spring from anywhere: your childhood, a particular color palette, or a burning desire for the mood of a different decade or place.

Ten years ago, a well-known Los Angeles photographer found a Frank Lloyd Wright tea set lost in a shuffle of dusty objects at the Rose Bowl flea market. The photographer bought it for $80. Long a fan of the Arts and Crafts movement of the early 1900s, he had been drawn to the tea set's seductive linear beauty. The artisan's identifying marks on the back confirmed the photographer's suspicions. Weeks later the tea set was appraised for $30,000.

However, these sorts of highly personal treasures may not be the only things you'll want. Like many of the other shoppers roaming up and down the ramshackle aisles of obscure flea markets, you'll probably want to keep your eye out for well-priced, well-made utilitarian goods. Many of these utilitarian basics have developed a ravenous following. So many people want these classics that it's fair to say that these well-designed items are now the raging must-have objects of desire. Vintage Depression glass, artware pottery, and flea market staples like cheerful fifties tablecloths now frequently appear to jazz up a tabletop. Their numerous appearances in decorating magazines only fan the fires.

Baby boomers know how the subliminal marketing of magazines works better than anybody. A national lust for simplicity (and stuff) means you won't be the only one who wants a matching luncheon set of Depression glass, a 1970s hand-blown Chemex drip coffee pot, or Yellow ware bowls. Especially if they appear, say, in *Martha Stewart Living.*

Spotting a trend before it's a trend can be very important. Being among the first to identify a seismic caliber trend is a coup known as having *the eye.* However, professionals acclaimed for having the eye also know there is slightly more to it than the luck of the draw.

The eye is a product of innate curiosity and is usually attached to the head that keeps an ear to the ground. It also takes a keen nose: the better to smell the salt when a sea change is in the air. A swing can happen at any time. For example, classic 1940s goods looked good until the war was over—then everyone wanted a future without a past. Atomic energy–era prints, kidney-shaped coffee tables, and bongo drums came— and went—and they are now yours for the plucking.

The more you know, the better your eye and your nose. Developing your intuitive senses will open up an amazing new world. Begin by asking dealers about anything that interests you. And once you're hooked on an era or a designer, go to art museums, historical museums, pier shows, and auctions to do your research. Study old newsreels or read books.

For instance, if your aesthetic leans toward the mellow colors, glazed or earthen finished pottery, rectilinear lights, or even the brass fixtures from the Arts and Crafts movement, you may want to learn to recognize details like the distinctive identifying chisel marks artisans used on hardware fixtures. Should your taste run to an entire decade (and not a specific collectible), you can use your VCR for a close-up. For example: if you're psychically drawn to the '60s, rent movies like *Petulia*, *Help!*, or *Dr. No*. Watch reruns of '60s television classics like *Hullabaloo*, *Man From U.N.C.L.E.*, or *The Avengers*.

Stop, pause, rewind. Observe the furniture, the rugs, the colors. You're looking for the details of a defining moment. The clothing they wore for the big scenes. The kinds of objects they placed on their coffee tables. Surfing a generation's favorite movies can help you recognize the perfect mod color scheme when you see it, begin a love affair with Rya rugs, or develop a need for a lava lamp of your very own.

If you're a 1950s furniture fan, don't miss a chance to rent Jacques Tati's 1958 classic *Mon Oncle*, Jack Lemmon's *Under the Yum-Yum Tree,* or just about any movie with Troy Donahue, Jayne Mansfield, or Connie Stevens. The idealized interiors are fascinating, and they will give you great insight into the lines, shapes, color combinations, and the vision of the times. It's great visual information, especially now that so many 1950s household goods are flooding the flea market scene as their owners retire to warmer climates.

However, resurrect the thing and to a certain extent you have to resurrect the ritual—since a lot of old stuff was passed down through the generations with a few instructions. From simple conventions that dictated placing insect-shaped estate jewelry pins on the shoulders of dresses and suits to rituals centered on maintenance. Fountain pens, for instance, need to be cleaned and refilled on a regular basis. Excess lighter fluid must be burned off when early model Zippo lighters are refilled, otherwise an inherent leak problem causes any excess fluid to burn right through pants' pockets.

Valuable secrets like these were usually passed on by fathers, college roommates, or Army buddies. But nowadays you have to quiz dealers or go on-line for maintenance tidbits.

In addition to learning about the specific attributes of any object, consider geography. For example, if you're just now developing a love for hotel silver, flow blue china, or Stickley furniture, you will pay top dollar in a picked-over field. Research can help increase your odds. The more you learn about any given genre or object, the more you'll know about where to look to find it the most economically.

Climate can be a giveaway when you're on the trail of a particular object. Different climates require different clothes and goods. Think Aspen consignment shops versus their Florida counterparts. Which one would be most likely to have great vintage sweaters? Or think about the people who move to Florida and decide their dark wood furniture looks out of place—you might pay bargain prices on mahogany.

Developing a knack for connecting lifestyles to aesthetics can take a little common sense—or a lot. Once you actually look into a category, you'll be amazed at how fast you can master its idiosyncracies. For example, as we approach the millennium there is a surplus of materials from the 1950s showing up everywhere—its because people who furnished their houses in the early 1950s are now retiring. You'll figure out why religious artifacts are often most prevalent in urban blue-collar, working-class cities with strong religious values and large immigrant populations like Baltimore or Pittsburgh. You'll rapidly conclude that parts of the country rich with attic- and basement-style houses yield far more "finds" than states known for single story "slab" houses, which must import all their flea market goods.

X-Finds

Sometimes you find your own special miracle with value and beauty apparent only to you.

New York makeup artist Robin Gaines tells the story of a find she made in Kingston, New York, while exploring a junk store called Eddy's that was jammed to the rafters with refrigerators, street lamps, bathtubs, and automobile parts. A lamp that looked like it had been made in a high school shop class caught her eye. The head wobbled and the proportions were weird at best. Even at fifty cents she passed on it. A week later, still obsessed by the funny-looking lamp on the top shelf, Robin drove back for a second look. Still, she couldn't figure out why she was fascinated by it.

Three weeks later she went back again, bought it, and turned it over. On the bottom she found her name, "Robin," burned into the wood. Another life? A missing twin? You be the judge.

Maybe it's all just a riff on the theory of racial memory that Djuna Barnes proposed in *Nightwood*. The theory holds that who we were in a previous life will cause us to be mysteriously drawn to objects or places that help us remember who we were at a different time, in a different place. Maybe . . .

Common sense can also lead you to the kinds of subtle insights that allow you to go straight to the source, thus eliminating the markup middleman. Take classic mid-century modern Scandinavian furniture. This genre is also known as "professor's furniture" because university faculty members embraced the aesthetic when it first came out, and more importantly, they lacked the money to replace it with newer styles as the years passed. So it shouldn't be too surprising that intact sets of 1950s Scandinavian furniture often turn up in university town flea venues before finding their way to more sophisticated urban pier and antique shows.

In many instances proximity matters the most. Because the Roycroft and Stickley furniture factories were located in upstate New York, amazing Arts and Crafts furniture turns up repeatedly in upstate New York, east of Buffalo. Collectibles from New Mexico's atomic past show up in relatively nearby Santa Fe flea markets because of their proximity to Los Alamos. Great electric fans often surface in Missouri because many were manufactured in St. Louis.

Other times, particularly on the international level, trading, settlers, and immigration swings make for fascinating displaced finds. For instance, Indonesia is a great source of early Modernist Dutch furniture and decorations. And Australia is so singularly situated as to be a gold mine for all kinds of Asian textiles, Tiffany bric-a-brac, and underpriced furniture from almost every port of call imaginable, many of which turn up in estate sales as well as flea markets. Bauhaus surfaces in Rio de Janeiro with frequency, while Nairobi auction houses repeatedly turn up great English and Danish pieces.

Whether you're looking in this country or abroad, any time you find a decade or a category that captures your imagination you'll find there are an enormous number of books available filled with the kind of information that can help you hunt down your prey. If you find it easier to learn through dialogue, you'll be amazed at how many objects have their own newsletters and annual meetings.

Going on-line will provide you with many opportunities to peruse, query, and learn. One good place to start is an Internet newsgroup named rec.antiques.marketplace where collectors meet to browse and haggle. The America Online Flea Market allows you to talk directly to dealers as well as regular people with something to sell. You'll also want to search the Antique Collectors Internet Directory at www.curioscape.com. (Or see the last chapter of this book!)

There has been a slew of news bulletins lately about fakes at flea markets. The truth is that you are just as likely to get something you like, and that the dealer doesn't know has a pedigreed provenance, as you are to be tricked. That said, remember dealers are in business to get top dollar. They work hard to get their stock and most have connections to shops and individuals who specialize and make a living based on their knowledge—yet sometimes your dealer has been duped as well. Even if you're certain what you're holding isn't an authentic tortoiseshell letterbox, don't expect the dealer to respond to your expertise. The market rules—and so does ego.

Stick to things you genuinely love within your price range and you'll never feel rooked.

If you're playing in the over $500 market, you might as well spend the time and effort necessary to learn to spot fakes. You'll not only save yourself from becoming paranoid about being taken—thus ruining a wonderful afternoon at a pier show—but you'll develop a deepened appreciation for authenticity.

To develop a veteran buyer's *savoir faire* and confidence, nothing beats a hands-on feel for the category of objects you're excited about, whether it's Depression glass or art pottery. The only way you'll know approximately how heavy the real thing really is to physically handle as many top quality authentic items as you can. For example, fake Tiffany lamps don't weigh nearly as much as the real thing. A fine wool feels very different than an average wool, but you'd be surprised how many of them are sold as authentic because the buyers haven't spent enough time getting a feel for the real thing.

You need to see what the colors are really like. Are they true, muddy, or translucent? Is the texture rough or smooth?

Depression glass turns up many fakes that don't have nearly the vibrancy of the real thing.

Wear patterns are also very important. Study both the exterior and the back of the object you like. Is that bureau you're pondering distressed enough to have been around since the year it was allegedly made? If it's not and you love it anyway, simply try to get a better price—but don't imagine it's an investment!

Auctions with free admissions are great places to learn all kinds of things. There are plenty to choose from: country auctions, estate auctions, even international auction houses, but best of all, when you go to an auction house, written information is usually available. Auction catalogs can be very educational, even if you're not there to buy. Just remember, the larger the auction house, the more accurate the description of any object. For example, Sotheby's is known for actually *guaranteeing* its catalog descriptions! If you're thinking of bidding at an auction, check to see if there are any footnote disclaimers about the validity of the descriptions.

In any case, if you are exploring the alter-economy for big league purchases, it pays to know as much about the real thing as you can—especially the price range. If the price is too good to be true and the dealer not only claims to know what it is but all about the artisan or manufacturer—you should be more than a little suspicious. For example: if someone tells you it's an authentic George Ohr pot which can sell for as much as $700 and they'll "let you have it for $100 because it's about to rain," be smart and walk away.

flea markets
Are Only the Beginning

CHAPTER **3**

A few years ago,

if you wanted well-made furniture or housewares and you weren't willing to pay for antiques,

you went to a flea market or possibly a junk store. As this decade ends, you have a few more options.

The alter-economy has expanded to include not just flea markets and junk stores, but antiques and collectibles shows, pier shows, seasonal shows, markets put on by town consortiums, twentieth-century antique boutiques, resale shops, auction houses, auction warehouses, estate sales, and the Internet. In short, you have a remarkable number of choices and adventures to choose from.

The Name Game

The generic names of these alter-economy venues are generally site-specific. Barn sales are held in barns. Garage sales are held in garages. Yard sales are held on yards. Tag sales are held inside houses, and the goods that are for sale have tags on them. Flea markets, however, can be called everything from trade days to swap meets.

If saving money is a major criteria, start your search for goods the same way a picker or a dealer would—at barn, garage, yard, and tag sales. Each has its own set of guidelines and opportunities, some of which are immediately obvious, many of which aren't.

Estate Sales

Estate sales are amazing sources of great things. So, it's too bad, there will be fewer and fewer *major* estate sales as the twentieth century proceeds—at least in this country. In fact, economists could practically plot an exponential curve to dictate to a certainty how many true estates are left to be disposed of and what surprises may be in them. Auction houses, however, are still the place to go for traditional well-to-do estate sales.

On the other hand, headline caliber estate sales aren't the only estate sales being advertised. If you think all those

"Estate Sale" listings in your local newspaper connote antiques only—surprise! Few of them are actually estates anymore, at least not in the grand sense of the word. Often they are held at the home of the original owner, and are not that different from tag sales.

In contemporary vernacular "Estate Sale" is now shorthand for all the goods the average person accumulates in a lifetime like clothes, dishes, furniture, appliances, lawn mowers, luggage, and occasionally antiques. If you do find one that is being held at the actual home, then get there early. The first ten early birds standing in line when the door opens usually get the proverbial worm.

In the case of the traditional estate sales held at auction houses there are usually ways to buy the goods that aren't prestigious. Call your local auction house to find out if they have a warehouse where everything that's not of exceptional quality ends up. Many of them do. These black holes are well worth sifting through to find everything from baby carriages to refrigerators. However, one word of caution. Some of these warehouses are a real mess, so don't suit up the way you might for an exclusive indoor evening auction.

If you decide to go to an auction house to bid at an estate or consignment sale, don't forget to bring a valid photo ID in order to get a bidding number. Plus, before you bid, always find out if you'll be charged a premium in the form of a surcharge added to the total amount of your purchases.

Antique Malls

If you want to shop for antiques and collectibles (without being exposed to either discount goods that pervade traditional flea markets, or the crowds that compete at auctions) you might want to explore a few antique malls. Antique malls are a new venue that has emerged in the last decade to meet the demands of enthusiastic twentieth-century collectors who want to shop during the week as well as on weekends. Basically they combine the stability and convenience of a normal store with the changing merchandise of a flea market. They are the fastest growing category in retail merchandising. They've sprung up everywhere from the poshest suburbs of Los Angeles to a Route 19 strip mall in Florida.

Antique malls sell goods from many individual dealers—but without the dealers being present. About all you'll run into is a cashier—which may be why they invariably make you check your handbag in a locker. Unfortunately it also means there is no one to ask whether a stain on the dress is recent or for more details on the provenance of what looks like a Chase cocktail shaker.

One big advantage of shopping at an antique mall, however, is that the quality of the goods at antique malls is usually pretty consistent. Plus, there is usually a broad selection of fairly well-edited stuff, all the better for not being exposed to the elements and from being packed and unpacked for days at a time. In addition, antique malls are open during the week as well as on weekends, and they usually take credit cards.

For ultimate quality flea goods, look to a relatively new genre of antique shops, which either specialize in one basic category or a well-edited mix. Shops that specialize amass the best of a single category like antique globes, retro-kitchenware, '50s *moderne,* or antique hardware fixtures. They offer goods that are usually excellent and sell them at "book price."

Boutiques with a "mix" rely on the owner's ability to assimilate and stay ahead of a range of popular trends. Whether the owner artfully mixes Hoosier cabinets, dressers, tramp art, pottery, and vintage tablecloths—or '50s wall units, pole lamps, and vintage chemistry beakers—the store's eclectic juxtapositions are part of its aesthetic. What is for sale hinges on the strength and editing of the boutique owner's taste and his or her area of expertise. Merchandise at these stores usually changes frequently. Each piece in the store is hand chosen by the owner, who possesses distinctive personal style or has great knowledge of either the era or the particular goods.

Whether you can afford to shop at these new boutiques of used goods or not, go to see as many of them as you can whenever possible. You'll develop a much faster read of what constitutes mint condition—and you'll get a surprising sense of what looks good with what—especially in shops that create vignettes. These small arranged tableaux are particularly helpful in letting you see just how much mileage you can get from a small space. You'll also be able to pick up some decorating tips.

One more bonus. When you find one of these boutiques, you'll usually find another. They are usually quite small and they tend to cluster. Take a walk along Lafeyette and Bond streets near SoHo when you're in New York City. Try the 7300 block of Beverly Boulevard in Los Angeles or King Street in Charleston.

Consignment Stores

Think of consignment shops as chic pawn shops. But even in die-hard yuppie strongholds (and especially in some yuppie strongholds), these stores have become immensely popular. They sell everything from barely worn designer clothing to very modern furniture. Some specialize in one category like clothing or furniture, others don't.

Flea Markets

There is no such thing as a plain old flea market. Each one is different. They can go all the way from dusty acres of tables selling discounted tube socks and T-shirts to fields of vintage miracles.

Flea markets also come in every denomination imaginable. There are weekly flea markets, monthly flea markets, seasonal flea markets, roadside flea markets, and weekday flea markets. Each one has its own fascinating set of pluses—and minuses. The most uncivilized—and some say the best—markets are the weekday markets which are primarily held for dealers and are usually held on Mondays. They begin before dawn as the dealers are unpacking. (A flashlight is crucial.)

If you are not fond of planning ahead, you know why weekend flea markets have become a fixture across the country. Although most of the people who attend them stop by as rarely as once a month, at least they get to pick the weekend themselves. If you do go as often as once a month, however, you'll notice the merchandise can get a little stale, since the dealers don't have as much time to scavenge for new things to sell. Weekly markets attract a range of dealers, so try to get a sense of which dealers are regulars and which aren't. This is useful if you need to resolve a problem like a vintage appliance that doesn't work, since you know you'll see the same dealer next week. (While they are under no obligation, a dealer who works the same market every week will be more likely to make some sort of restitution than a dealer who works the market only erratically.)

Monthly flea markets are almost always held at an inside location during the winter. In the summer they are almost all held both indoors *and* outdoors. They tend to offer the most upscale merchandise. You'll also notice if you start to go regularly that the good ones attract the same dealers every month with only a small percentage of transient dealers. Local dealers tend to have a handle on what people are looking for, which means they often sell more interesting things.

Roadside flea markets tend to be as hit-or-miss as garage sales. You can find damaged, ramshackle goods, or occasionally you might find something quite fascinating. The latter is why flea pioneers never rule them out entirely.

Seasonal flea markets have become the Meccas of the alter-economy. They are markets that are held two to three times a year. The well-known seasonals are almost always exclusively "antiques and collectibles"–caliber events with a low tube sock quotient. They are also more expensive as a rule. However, if you are persistent and lucky, you could negotiate a true bargain by Sunday afternoon of the last day.

Junk Stores

If the thrill of being the one to find "it" is as important to you as owning it—or if your taste runs to funkier objects than might turn up in a more edited establishment—try visiting a few junk stores in your area until you find one with possibilities.

No matter how idiosyncratic, inconsistent, and even messy they may be at first glance, finding a great junk store is like discovering the single best table at an entire flea market. Stores like Haywire in Los Angeles (across the street from the Raleigh Studios) or Sammy's in New York City's SoHo district are deservedly legendary for being packed to the gills with desirable stuff from every decade and category: weird lamps, aquarium toys, Hollywood souvenirs, 1950s sculptures, voodoo goods, bar stools, and the list goes on.

Unlike newer antique boutiques, where the store owners pride themselves on their ability to artfully choose and edit their choices, most junk store proprietors rarely discriminate on the basis of quality or trendiness—which is why the majority of junk stores fall into the category of hit-or-miss garage sales. Professional pickers love them because there can be so much stuff buried on the back of shelves or in boxes out back that the whiff of a miracle find is always in the air. In fact, the remote promise of the obscure object tucked away on the back shelf is why junk stores continue to remain a solid link in the new antique food chain—especially if the price sticker hasn't been updated in the last decade. In a junk store, it's up to you to see the possibilities. Stay open-minded as you scan the helter skelter mixes of slightly stained tablecloths, dog-eared books, teapots, mildewed magazines, and crates of old records.

Home Shopping

Any time you find a dealer who works out of his or her house, stop the car—especially in the Midwest. You'll find these dealers don't always keep up with the latest prices, and better yet, their overhead is lower than shop owners or dealers in antique malls.

Pawn Shops

Pawn shops are one of the oldest links in the alter-economy food chain, and their cult following is growing. Any time you're hunting for musical instruments, cameras, or diamond rings with a history, don't overlook your local pawn shop. Pawn shops are always an interesting guide to what's going on in the economy, in specific subcultures, and in your neighborhood.

One Florida drug lawyer swears pawn shops are an amazingly accurate reflection of what drug dealers invested in five to ten years ago. (If that's the case, Thai gold medallions appear to have been considered quite a blue chip investment.) Other armchair visionaries see pawn shops fast becoming a barometer of former '80s yuppie addictions like Rolex watches, Minolta cameras, opera binoculars, and the like.

Shows

There are small shows, major shows, and more and more shows in the middle. Some are dedicated to a single era or col-

lectible, some are high-level clan gatherings of antique dealers, and some are basically monthly flea markets that no
longer call themselves flea markets.

On the high end, a show consists of a number of professional
dealers who meet in the same place at the same time every
year. What they sell is calculated to appeal to decorators and
relatively serious collectors. Everything offered is invariably in
mint condition and special. Twentieth-century shows, for
example, are a great opportunity to see everything from a
perfect '60s Chemex coffee maker to the very best of the
industrial designer furniture collections, flatware, and one-of-
a-kinds.

In addition to general era shows, there are also special collection shows that range from specific kinds of art pottery to
Western collectibles. Many of them do charge, but they're
usually worth it in order to see the best or simply to get an
education.

Tag Sales

Tag sales offer the entire contents of a house: furniture, clothing, tools, trinkets, toys, whatever—and while some are run
by the home owner, more often they're run by professional
consultants who are paid on commission. These professionals
price goods based on their experience and knowledge of the

market and they're rarely as flexible as the original owner unless it has been a very slow day. Everything with a tag on it is up for grabs—and grabs is the operative word unless it's tagged "Not For Sale" (often abbreviated NFS). By the way, if you spot something you're interested in at a tag sale, carry it around with you until you make up your mind. Tag sales, yard sales and estate sales can all be very competitive environments.

Town Pick-Up Days

Your town has one. It's that one day a month designated for large trash pick-up and it's when you and everyone else pulls the big stuff out to the curb. Some towns even have regularly scheduled coffee klatches near the local dump with craft tables! Not only can you find extravagantly rusted water heaters at the trash dump (sculpture fixings in the right hands) but you'll also find dining room chairs, bed frames, vintage bureaus, and sleds.

Better yet, if your neighbor's trash isn't exactly what you had in mind, go international. Trash pick-up day is an institution from Milan to Bavaria.

Yard Sales, Garage Sales, Barn Sales, Etc.

These are held everywhere from the posh Hamptons and Beverly Hills to the less glamorous front stoops in Brooklyn. Usually, they are one-time events held by people who are trying to simplify their lives, move, or clean out the garage. Depending on the neighborhood or the county they can be well worth your while.

This particular branch of the alter-economy has spawned a great new chain of events in which whole communities and even entire highways of communities come together to hold annual sales along a particular route or in a community center. Some of these mutual events are already becoming legends— like the 450-Mile Flea Market in Kentucky.

basic
SURVIVAL
Skills 101

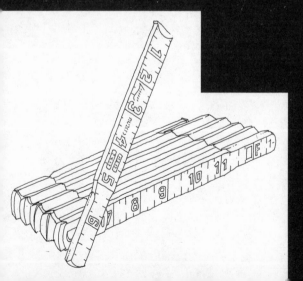

Shopping in the alter-economy tests your primal hunting and gathering skills. So, as with any adventurous undertaking, it helps if you know the lay of the land and bring the right tools.

Half of your tool box is in your head. The best tool you own is attitude. Strive to **be tough**. You don't need to buy everything you see. Discipline yourself not to buy anything that needs repair (unless it only needs refinishing), is missing a piece, or you simply don't need. **Be nonchalant**. It does you no good to appear needy—especially if you want to get a great price. Having a **great sense of humor** helps as well—or at least the philosophy that everything works out for the best eventually. You'll need it for all those times you walk away to think about a space alien model kit and it's gone when you return ten minutes later.

The rest of the tools you need you already have around your house or are easy enough to get your hands on.

A **newspaper** is a must. In particular the classified section. Weekend ads usually begin running on Thursday, which gives you plenty of time to organize your itinerary. You can find barn sales, yard sales, even lawn sales in the classified section of almost any newspaper, or try special weekly shopping publications that are basically compilations of classifieds. Look under headings like "Auctions and Sales," "For Sale by Owner," or "Yard Sales." To locate tag sales, look for eye-catching headlines like "Blow-Out Blastorama" or "Bargain Blitz!"

Read between the lines. Classified headlines are alive with subtext. For example, the heading "Colonial Treasures." It usually means traditional sofas, spinning wheel planters, brass lamps, etc. If that look is useful to you, hula on over—as early as possible. Conversely, if you're not a fan of the genre, don't bother to set the alarm.

When you see the word "housewares" in a classified ad, it means small items like cookware, dishes, and lamps. When you see "household goods" it means the owner is selling large items like appliances and furniture. So if you're on the lookout for a couch, don't waste time with houseware sales. Head off in search of bigger game.

Don't overlook the heading "Moving Sales" either. These events can turn up treasure trove material, especially if you live in an area like Washington, D.C.—or near any Army base or military installation where embassy personnel and career Army families on the move often sell amazing things from exotic countries, as well as VCRs, mattresses, and couches. "Divorce Sales" can be bonanzas as well.

If you find yourself regularly beaten to the punch by hordes of other eager junkers (and dealers) try this old dealer's trick. After you've gone through the classifieds and made your list for the weekend, circle the most desirable ads in the classifieds, then prioritize your list from the most promising sale to the least promising sale. Then instead of driving directly to the most promising, start at the least promising, proceed to the next least promising, etc. Save the one that sounds the best for last. Since this is the opposite direction than the one everyone else will move in you'll increase your odds of having first pick of the litter from at least one of the yard sales.

Don't forget to think big. Even if you're a budget-conscious yard sale shopper, don't overlook the special antique shows that are advertised in your local newspaper's Home and/or Weekend section, plus its Sunday events calendar. Once you start noticing the listings for them, you'll be amazed at the number of pier shows, vintage fashion expos, antique and collectible shows, Art Deco shows, Art Nouveau shows, Western shows, collector shows, auctions, and special estate sales that go on every weekend across the country. These shows are usually fun—as well as educational. (Art and antique magazines are also a valuable resource if you are curious about the high end of the market. They usually have **a calendar of special events** in the back that lists special events all across the country and internationally.)

These calendars come in handy, because special events take place all over the country virtually all the time. Even if the goods cost more than they might if you found them at a yard sale or a flea market, events and special shows are an ideal way to get a hands-on feel for truly great collectibles, acquire a few tips on what's interesting, and spot trends in the making. You can also find an exhaustive listing of newsletters and publications by category in a book called *Maloney's Antiques and Collectibles Resource Directory*, by David Maloney Jr. (Serious junkers, decorators, and stylists subscribe to *Antiques and the Arts Weekly* newspaper published by The Bee Publishing Company in Newton, Connecticut.)

Newspapers, bulletin boards, and magazines, for all their value, can never replace the **Yellow Pages**, which may be the definitive guide to the alter-economy. Look under "Thrift Shops," "Auctioneers," and "Flea Markets." Whether you're on vacation or in your own home town, those ubiquitous Yellow Pages can lead to some very interesting adventures.

Once you are alert to the myriad possibilities it's amazing how many alter-economy venues you'll notice wherever you go. For example, scan your local supermarket or Laundromat **community bulletin board**. It's an ever changing gold mine of church bazaars, yard sales, garage sales, and fund raising flea markets. (Just be sure and check the dates carefully; notices aren't always taken down as regularly as they should be.)

Other helpful tools depend on your needs. If your idea of a miracle find is a decorative coup for your living room, bring along **fabric swatches** and a **tape measure**, as well as notations of any crucial dimensions. Or take a minute to measure your foot and the span of your hand—that way you'll always have a rough idea of an object's dimensions no matter when or where you find something special.

Carry a **magnet**. It will stick to cheap base metals or iron—but it won't stick to bronze, copper, brass, silver, or steel. A magnet comes in very handy if you're in the market for silver candlesticks. (Or 1930s Chase Specialty pieces, which were never made of chromium plated steel—therefore never magnetic.) If you're looking for art pottery or silver and you need to get a good look at hallmarks or flaws, bring a **magnifying glass**. Some collectors even look carefully at patent information!

Carry a business or personal **card** with you to give a dealer in case you find one who shares your taste and is willing to keep an eye out for the special thing you're trying to find. (However once you alert a dealer to the fact that you're a collector, you should probably expect to pay a higher price.) You can also ask dealers if they know anyone else who might carry what you're looking for, since dealers do tend to know a lot of other dealers.

Keep a **notebook** and pen in your pocket. If a dealer's taste and mix appeal to you, note his or her phone number *and* the objects you coveted. When you start to torture yourself over a drafting table from the early 1900s that you walked away from two weeks ago, you can light a candle and call to see if maybe, just maybe . . .

Die-hard "documentarians" also use their notebooks to record descriptions of new purchases, including dimensions, color, cost, and any history of it they can learn from the dealer. (This will be useful—if not invaluable—information in case you ever decide to resell the thing you just bought.) If you're really serious about collecting you can transfer the information to file cards and organize them by category. There is even a **computer software program** made by the Dinmark Group called CollectorPro that lets you catalog your purchases and build a database of your collectibles right down to the pattern, date acquired, asking price, price paid, condition, etc.

Yard sale addicts usually carry a good **street map** in their glove compartment. Even if you know exactly how to find the one yard sale you've circled in the classifieds, it's amazing how many others you will see signs for on the way to the one you marked. Often these detours are even better than the sale you were trying to find—which is part of what makes the day an adventure, but finding your way home without your trusty map can be a bit of a challenge.

Never go to any major flea market without **toilet paper**. Keep a length in your pocket if you're going to any of the big seasonal markets like Brimfield. You'll be lucky to find a portable toilet without a long line—much less toilet paper.

Keep **old blankets**, **bubble wrap**, and the like in your trunk. You'll be lucky to get a plastic bag or even an old newspaper from a dealer to wrap your latest flea market or yard sale acquisition. If you're on the lookout for ceramics, glass, or even furniture, be sure and store old blankets—or even the plastic cushioned pads they sell for bedwetting—in the trunk of your car. They will help you carefully protect your find on the way home. (If you're on an oversized furniture buying mission, you may even want to buy moving blankets from a local mover or hardware superstore.)

When's the Best Time to Go?

The big question is invariably whether to arrive at daybreak or not.

If you're *serious,* arrive early. The very best goods go first—giving early birds with flashlights first dibs. Professional dealers, store owners, and people looking for furniture arrive at dawn.

If you're not that serious, sleep in. Noon is just fine. But keep in mind that if you are in a state with miserably hot weather, outdoor markets (even those with covered pavilions) tend to be over by noon—no matter what the posted hours claim. Prices, on the other hand, go up and down all day long.

Unlike international markets, particularly in Asia and the Middle East, where the first sale of the day is low because it's supposed to generate good luck, in American markets during the opening hours, optimism and higher prices run rampant. Rudimentary dealer logic says if a customer shows great interest in an imaginative 1940s Lucite handbag at 7 A.M., why sell it for less than the sticker price? The dealer has all day to find someone else who is not only just as interested in quirky accessories as you are, but who might meet the asking price without a second thought.

On the other hand, not all dealers are such generalists that they know what *everything* is worth. They need to talk to other dealers who may know more about some of their latest acquisitions than they do. So until they have set up *and* had sufficient time to wander around and ask other dealers what's what and what it's worth, a dealer's first-thing-in-the-morning sticker price can be unexpectedly low.

Often, if you don't get there first, the same object will be sold by one dealer to another and another and another and marked up accordingly. In fact, many objects bunny hop between dealers at the same market on the same day.

At the end of the day (especially on the last day of a seasonal flea market), the goods may be picked over, but prices can be rock bottom because dealers would rather sell something than pack it up again.

A strategy worth trying if you're even slightly ambivalent about the object in question is to arrive early, find a find, decide you can live without it although you'd really rather not abandon it, and then return at the end of the day to see if it is still there. If it is, your odds of acquiring the piece for a song greatly increase.

Midday junkers should always take a good, long look around. If no one appears to be buying, you either missed the great stuff altogether, or it's a slow day and you have a bargaining edge. You should be able to size this up quickly.

The one time you must arrive early is at auctions. You need to have time to inspect the merchandise very carefully. Those well-publicized returns at the Jacqueline Kennedy Onassis auction were practically the first in history for any customers other than regulars with an extensive history with the auction house.

More than anything, you need to have **a plan of action** when you go to a big flea market. It can make all the difference. Any time you are wandering around a big market like Brimfield, Sandwich, or one of the Renningers, logistics can slow you down if you start at the beginning. Try starting at the booth furthest from the parking lot and then work your way back, keeping track of your route. Bread crumbs, anyone?

Naturally, it's very easy to get distracted from your original game plan, but if you **start as far back** as possible before you get distracted—you'll see more *and* find more time to spend at the tables you enjoy the most. Plus you'll have first shot at the least picked over tables since most shoppers start at the tables nearest the entrance! Walk as quickly as possible, scanning as you go, so you'll get a sense of which aisles you can ignore. Otherwise you'll find yourself loaded down and miles from your car, just as you're getting warmed up.

Haggling Made Human

Never forget to be grateful to the vagabond spirit in those who assemble and caravan odd stuff for your benefit. In other words, a little light bargaining is fun but don't get too rapacious. It can take the edge off the day for everyone.

That said, when it comes to prices, a lot of people believe there are no more bargains left, that everyone in America knows the value to the penny of every semi-antiquity in his or her cupboard. Could be, but in the alter-economy, your enjoyment is the great unknown and that gives you the home court advantage. So here are the rules—if you can call them that.

Thrift shops rarely bargain and neither do consignment shops, although it never hurts to ask, and both of these venues are known for holding half-off sales. (Get yourself on their mailing lists.) If you want to give it a try, recognize that the best way to bargain is to find a reason to pay less—like a flaw—and the best way to negotiate is to convince yourself you don't need it.

Antique malls will usually call the dealer for you to
see if he or she will accept a lower price or give you
10 percent off with a decorator's number. Some
dealers even have a built-in 10 percent discount
available to absolutely anyone who inquires. (But
generally speaking, these edited venues operate
more like stores and less like flea markets.) If it's a
time of year when tourists rarely visit the area,
always have the antique mall manager call the dealer
for a specific item or cluster of items to ask if they
can "do better for you." (Many shoppers, by the way,
believe that depending on location and time of year,
antique malls offer better prices than some flea
markets.)

Remember cash is still the coin of the realm at most
flea markets, but credit cards are beginning to be
accepted with the advent of antique malls, special
antique shows, and continually evolving venues.
(Many dealers will let you pay by check, but be
prepared to show the same ID you would show in a
store.) Unless you are prepared to pay in cold hard
cash, it's best to call ahead and ask if you have any
other options.

At flea markets, pier shows, yard, estate, and tag
sales, the sticker price is not necessarily the final
price. There is always a dealer's price. Getting to it is
the problem. What you think the dealer paid for the
object is irrelevant. The actual selling price is
determined by what you, or someone else, is willing to
pay—and how the day is going. On a slow day if you
demonstrate even remote interest in an object, the
seller will usually approach you to say the price is
negotiable. If five people are clustered around the

table, count on paying the asking price—unless you are buying in quantity.

When you are at a flea market, tag sale, thrift, or resale shop, don't get too exuberant crowing over an exceptional find before you've purchased it—you'll attract the competition. And don't go out of your way to tell the dealer that the $10 print you've just acquired actually belongs in a retrospective at the National Museum of Art. (After all, you may wish to buy again from the same dealer.)

Consider keeping reference books on collectibles at home. The "book price" isn't as relevant to the price you can offer as you might think, unless you're at a very chic event. Book prices represent the price the ultimate collector for that particular object will pay. If you spot the same thing at a yard sale, a near-empty flea market, or at the end of the day we hope you will only pay a fraction of the book price.

Never overlook the bargaining power of clustering. If you are buying several objects, always group them—and then talk turkey—especially if you're paying over $40. Ask the dealer, "If I take these three things, what can you do for me?" (In international flea markets, where the tax can be as high as 18–20 percent, bargaining by quantity is vital!)

Before you make a bid, always scan the scene carefully. Is it crowded? Are other people buying? What time of day is it? What's the weather like? (Bad weather, by the way, can be your friend if it keeps the crowds away.) If you don't see many people carrying anything, it could be a slow day. The merchandise could be uninspiring. Or the prices could be sky high.

All of which can work in your favor if you find something you would like to buy. Because at the end of the day no flea market dealer wants to pack up *all* his or her merchandise.

But let's say you've only found one thing you must have: an old chair marked $20. It's late afternoon, the market is emptying out. Begin by asking the dealer if $20 is the "best price." If the dealer says he can do $15, try tactfully offering $8: "Would you be insulted if I offered you $8? It's all I have, and I'm not sure my second cousin for whom I'm buying it doesn't already own a similar chair." Chances are you'll get that $20 chair for $8. (Worst case scenario, $10.)

But no matter how compelling the object, remember your aim is to *bargain,* not browbeat, the dealer. The few dollars the dealer might make from the item will rarely encourage him or her to sell to someone determined to have a hostile transaction. If you've never bargained before, spend a few minutes eavesdropping. Listening to other people negotiate is a great way to get your sea legs. And if you don't get the price that feels right to you, it's always acceptable to say, "I'll pass."

One last crucial tip: Bring one-dollar bills if you're planning to become a serious bargainer. It's in poor taste to pull out a thick roll of twenties—especially if you have been quibbling over two or three dollars. It also helps you set a limit when you bring small bills. When they're gone, you're done for the day.

There is an unwritten dress code at flea markets. Serious junkers always wear **clothes with many pockets**. The better to stash aspirin and a cloth hat as well as a tape measure. They also seem to have an avid predilection for khakis and blue jeans. (Unless you're junking in New York, where vintage clothing is also popular for pre-dawn shopping raids). However, there is more to a flea market dress code than utilitarian considerations.

Think about the message you're sending before you head out to the playing field. Save your Breitling tank watch, your favorite Armani pantsuit, or even an extravagant wedding ring for an outing to the auction houses, where appearances actually can help you get more attention! Unless you are going to a flea market exclusively to meet people, there is literally nothing to be gained in looking affluent. You will only undermine your position. The look you're going for is **low key**.

As with any outdoor adventure, **never wear new shoes** to a big-time market that covers acres and acres. Pack a rain poncho, a sun hat, or whatever the weather suggests. Bring your own shopping or tote bag or better yet bring **a pull cart**. You can just keep on shopping till that cart is full rather than scuttling back and forth to your far away car with heavy purchases. At markets like the Rose Bowl in Pasadena, you'll see practically as many pull carts as you will in a New York City supermarket. (Pull carts are also an excellent place to stash the rain poncho or a light jacket if the weather looks iffy.)

However, the most important tool could be your **telephone**. Not all flea markets are great. Some of them are simply booth after booth of new discount goods. So call ahead and ask for the percentage of new goods to vintage and how many dealers will be there. (At least one hundred usually means it's a good market, depending on the new-to-used ratio.)

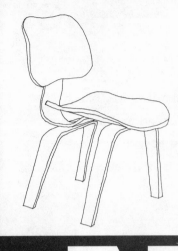

the

Now
FILE

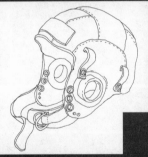

CHAPTER

Welcome to predawn *fin de siècle* shopping made simple.

Now you see it. Now you don't. Now you want it. Like any "best of" list, the Now File represents what taste-meisters in New York and Los Angeles covet. So don't just read it, feel free to trash it as a trend-o-fanatic laundry list—or use it as a treasure map to explore the plunder of the late twentieth century.

This is basically a now-what list. As in now that I've discovered my Aunt Lois has a dusty rose anodized aluminum Kool-Aid pitcher in her basement, do *I* need it, want it, *or what*?

Some of the things that made the cut are camp, kitsch, or even gay pop, but don't belittle them—their prices can surpass "antiques." Still others are in the process of ascending to antique status purely by the virtue of their age. Some of this stuff fell out of status because it was and is ugly. It remains ugly. It's simply back for more obscure reasons like nostalgia or the curious allure of truly bad taste.

Some things made the list because of their remarkable quality. For example, they simply don't make some appliances like they used to. The trick with many of the objects on the list is to imagine them in new contexts, new configurations, and new surroundings.

To me design is a way of discussing life. It is a way of discussing society, politics, eroticism, food, and even design. At the end, it is a way of building up a possible figurative utopia or metaphor about life. Certainly to me, design is not restricted to the necessity of giving form to a more or less stupid product for a more or less sophisticated industry.

—Ettore Sottsass, Italian industrial designer

> # Have nothing in your house that you do not know to be useful or believe to be beautiful.
>
> —**William Morris, mid-Victorian design reformer, poet, and Socialist**

AIRLINE ANYTHING

The sky's the limit when it comes to all kinds of airline collectibles. Think plastic model planes. Framed and matted photographs of planes. Aviation art. Stewardess uniforms. Blankets. Military wings. Civilian wings. The airline wings children collect. Desk or travel agency models of rockets, missiles, and sputniks. The snow globes they sold in the airline shops. Travel stickers. China, India, or Burma bracelets related to aviation. And naturally, Air Force anything.

ALUMINUM ANYTHING

These days aluminum rules. Aluminum is a machine-age medium that imparts a homespun yet curiously utilitarian look to canisters, tea kettles, salt and pepper shakers, as well as heavy, family-sized, polished aluminum Wagner farm-style tea kettles with wooden handles.

Polished *spun aluminum* from the '40s and '50s—particularly if it was designed by Russel Wright—is quite a coup. His early designs in spun aluminum include trays, vases, and teapots.

Anodized aluminum from the '50s is also moving up in desirability. Trendy dealers believe that lightweight, shiny colored aluminum pitchers in rose or blue, once used for Kool-Aid on a daily basis, are just about due for a major revival. Call your mother or grandmother to see if she still has hers.

Handwrought aluminum—also known as known as "poor man's silver" or "hammered aluminum"—is a distinctive 1950s pockmarked metal. It was once the preferred medium for chafing dishes, lazy Susans, nut bowls, platters, relish dishes, casseroles, cocktail shakers, trays, tiered trays, silent butlers, handbags, jewelry, and wastebaskets. Keep your eye out for pieces signed by Rodney Kent, Arthur Armour, and Wendall August. (Curiously, the fact that it's called handwrought aluminum means nothing in particular—the vast majority of aluminum was mass-produced, and proud of it.)

Caretaker #10

♣ If your breakable glass or ceramic collection sits on a shelf, a ledge, or up high, use a conservation wax like Quake Wax. Not exactly a glue, this indispensable soft wax was developed to keep breakable stuff in place in the midst of a mild earthquake or a slammed door. It never hardens and the object can be lifted by giving it a slight twist or running dental floss through the wax. Apply a few dots to the base of an object before you place it on a shelf or mantelpiece. However, should you lift an object up to show your friends how neat the stuff is, be sure and add a fresh layer when you put your treasure back where you found it.

If you can't find Quake Wax, use dental wax in a pinch. Your dentist should be able to supply it.

☆ Where there is smoke, you may need ozone. If you can't get the smell of vintage smoke from a fire or too many cigarettes out of clothes and textiles, then ozone cleaning is your only hope. Call the Neighborhood Dry Cleaning Association in New York to find the name of the nearest dry cleaner with an ozone machine.

❀ **Check references. If you need to restore an important piece, get referrals for experienced, reliable artisans from antique dealers. Never trust your furniture to anyone who can't show you other examples of their work.**

✳ Use the delicate cycle, a net bag, tepid water, and mild soap to wash vintage linens. Rinse everything at *least* twice to prevent rust spots and yellowing.

✱ **To clean and season an old or dirty cast-iron frying or roasting pan, rub it thoroughly with steel wool, rinse it, then fill it with oil. Heat the pan until the oil is very hot. Pour the oil out. Then repeat the process at least twice more. Pour some salt in the pan after you've poured out the last batch of oil, rub the salt in generously, and wipe it out. Fry up some bacon, and you have a fry pan that's seasoned and ready to use.**

☆ Use old newspapers to transport dishes from a flea market, but don't store them in newsprint for any great length of time. The newsprint ink can transfer and stain your china. Batting or blister wrap is a better idea.

✳ **To clean sporting goods, use a lanolin-based cleaner with a fine steel-wool pad and rub the wood bits with a bit of wax.**

✳ Smell books before you buy them. If you simply must have a leather-bound classic that is more than a little on the musty side, try this fume bath. Take a small plastic container (the kind you get from a deli) and fill it with wadded-up paper towels and ½ cup of bleach. Then, punch holes in the lid and close the plastic container. Next, put your book(s) in a heavy trash bag, sit the bleach container on top of the book(s), and seal the bag securely for twenty-four hours.

❧ **Clean tarnished or corroded brass with Lysol toilet bowl cleaner and extra fine steel wool. Don't forget to wear gloves.**

☆ To maintain the finish of stripped metal furniture, remember to industriously rub the surface with car or butcher's wax.

✱ **Rub vintage leather handbags with a cloth dipped in white vinegar to help restore the luster and to diminish tiny scratches.**

✳ If you're storing a carpet for a period of time, remember to roll it pile side out and then wrap it up with white sheets and moth balls.

✱ **Many dealers swear that the best thing to use on painted wood grain furniture is Scott's Liquid Gold.**

☆ If you store quilts, remember to take them out of the closet or trunk once a year and fold them differently so they won't get lines.

❧ **To get those hard-to reach crevices of glassware and vases clean, try filling them with a fizz cocktail of warm water and a denture-cleaning tablet.**

AMERICAN MODERN

A true home run. Manufactured by Steubenville, American Modern was the most popular dinnerware pattern ever designed. Created by revered industrial designer Russel Wright, his solid color shapes were strange for the times and the occasional pattern (like grass) was basically abstract, which was equally unusual. Even more astoundingly, the salt and pepper shakers didn't match by design. One might be bean brown and the other chartreuse. In short, it was *the* dinner set to own—the design breakthrough of the 1950s.

The most popular colors include black chutney, cantaloupe, cedar green, chartreuse, coral, glacier blue, granite gray, blue, seafoam, white—and bean brown.

ASHTRAYS & LIGHTERS

Now that ashtrays are becoming an endangered species, they're hot again. Especially oversized green Depression glass, chrome, glass, post-war Venini, or strange commemoratives. Hold out for a great one. Ashtrays may be endangered, but you still have quite a choice. Recycle them for utilitarian functions like holding keys, storing paper clips, or showcasing your marble collection.

Lighters are just as chic. Top of the line, ultradurable Ronson, Dunhill, or Evans coffee table and pocket lighters are practically art, while venerable, windproof, pre-1960 Zippo pocket lighters are just as hot. Serious loyalists hold out for vintage 1940s models, Vietnam models, and other commemorative models with a distinctive click. (Zippo Manufacturing Co. even annually holds their own giant swap meet on the grounds of their corporate headquarters in western Pennsylvania.)

When Is Silver Really Silver?

In order to be considered sterling, 925 parts out of 1,000 have to be made of silver. Oddly enough, having silver in the name is totally irrelevant when it comes to determining worth. For example, German silver—sometimes known for good reason as nickel silver—doesn't have a drop of silver in it. Ditto for Alaskan silver and Brazilian silver. So get a feel for the weight, patina, and luster of the real thing, and try to deal with reputable dealers or at least dealers who are at the same place every weekend.

BAKELITE

Its inventor, Dr. Leo Baekeland, called Bakelite the "material of a thousand uses." In its heyday, this pliable early plastic truly was. Best of all, this synthetic substance was the darling of industrial designers like Raymond Loewy. This meant it was used for every object imaginable from cocktail shakers to telephones and transistor radios, fountain pens, billiard balls, and radiator caps.

Beware of fakes. Real Bakelite has a slight smell of carbolic acid when you rub it hard and fast or heat it with hot water.

BARBED WIRE

These knotty metal strands can originate on a farm, a penitentiary, a military installation, or somewhere in the once-wild West. The number of knot patterns is amazing. Strange as it may sound, these days barbed wire turns up at flea markets quite regularly. It is usually collected in eighteen-inch lengths and displayed mounted on boards or matted and framed.

Should you get hooked, there are even clubs for barbed wire collectors and a periodical called the *Barbed Wire Collector* which is published in Lewisville, Texas.

BARN PULLEYS

Farmers once used barn pulleys to pull up heavy loads in barns—thus the name. They also carved and constructed these wood and metal "tools" by hand, which makes each one different and fascinating. Barn sales, auctions, and flea markets in the Midwest are your best bet for finding these beautifully aged, one-of-a-kind pieces of the past.

BAUER POTTERY

This California classic dinnerware resonates with charm and color. In fact, Mr. Bauer is widely credited for the term "California color." Bauer Pottery started in Los Angeles in 1939 to manufacture flowerpots. It wasn't until some ten years later that they began producing their dinnerware designs. Bauer ware is known for its simple ridged lines, wonderful serving pieces, and great colors with depth and a twist like chartreuse, olive green, glossy pastels, and a deep orange-red. (The black and the white pieces are the rarest.)

The Bauer name should be impressed on the bottom of each genuine piece. The firm closed in 1962. And if you're just starting a collection, you should be aware it's most prevalent on the West Coast.

BICENTENNIAL BOUNTY

Can't afford the real things from circa 1776?

Not to worry. You can relive the centennial again and again with all-American merchandise from the biggest marketing event of 1976. Special red, white, and blue mugs, plates, tea towels, framed invitations, silver-plated cake servers, etc. There's no way to miss these gaudy, patriotically decorated commemoratives when you see them. Your best bet for plugging the gaping hole in your 1976 stash is to check out estate and tag sales in Washington, D.C., and its surrounding environs.

BILLIARD & CUE BALLS

What's not to like? Old billiard balls have a worn, warm magical glow. They are evocative, round, and made in all your favorite numbers (one through nine) and colors (purple, blue, orange, red). Billiard balls from the early 1900s were made from Bakelite before they were made of plastic. (The oldest ones are ivory!)

Imagine them heaped in a bowl, under a glass dome, or left along a ledge.

BLACK & WHITE PHOTOGRAPHY

Look for evocative imagery: Hawaiian volcanoes, canoes, 1950s abandon, Ivy League crews, portraits, weddings, dogs, horses, or any other image that speaks to you. Don't worry about the original frame. It's the imagery that matters—and the size. Bigger is better.

When you remat and frame your newfound photographs, don't scrimp on the quality of the glass. You'll have memorable art that works in almost any environment.

BLANKETS

Vintage blankets look great layered over other printed blankets, mixed with trapunto quilts, stacked in multiples on shelves, or in summer house guest rooms.

The warming trend in blankets currently includes: heavy melton wool striped Pendleton blankets, Army blankets, commemorative blankets, camp blankets, and vintage reproduction trapper blankets—especially the ones with the black lines in the corner designating the number of beavers you needed to buy it.

CALLING CARDS

Once upon a time travelers brought home travel stickers, decals, and the occasional plastic landmark. Nowadays calling cards used to make long distance calls have captured the hearts of a new generation.

No wonder. Time flies—especially if it's long distance. And while calling cards have been around less than a decade, they already have an ardent following if they are well designed, and especially if they are European designs.

CARNIVAL GLASS

Once upon a time, fairs and carnivals gave this stuff away as prizes. Too bad we weren't there to win these trophies. Opaque, iridescent carnival glass was introduced in 1905 and stopped being produced by the 1930s. It symbolized a mega-watt break from the overbearing Victorian era.

Exotic chameleon colors flash from different angles in different lights. Because of all its colorful variations, Carnival glass is also known as taffeta glass and Etruscan glass. Flourishes like ruffles, crimping, inverted rims, and lacy, ornate patterns hide imperfections in the many patterns of dinnerware, glasses, and side dishes. Many people believe the opaque quality of carnival glass vases works better with flowers than clear glass.

It's also easy to find, although some colors are much rarer than others: especially red, pastel yellow green, and amber. Ice blue and green are rumored to now be giving brighter colors a run for their money in the popularity department.

What Makes a House a Home?

"Your stuff."

—Richard Mauro, president of Joan Vass USA

his collections:

Campaign furniture
Painted furniture
Pressed glass goblets
Bakelite flatware
Vintage handkerchiefs, pocket squares, and ties
Modern Library editions of classics from the '30s, '40s, and '50s
Monkeys
Black and white photography

CHASE PRODUCTS

The Chase Chrome and Brass Company was founded in 1870 and they are especially remembered for their Art Deco line. Nothing oozes Deco like Chase-designed chrome shapes (which don't need polishing). Chase specialties like coffee and tea sets, lamps, cocktail shakers, trays, pretzel stands, and plumbing supplies were the rage in the 1930s. No wonder;

they were designed by the likes of Russel Wright, Walter Van Nesson, Ruth Gerth and Harry Laylon, and Reiman.

Chase designers worked in chromium, brass, and copper, occasionally silver plate, and occasionally with Bakelite trim. Look under handles, in grooves, and other nooks for a small centaur with a drawn bow and the word "Chase" below.

CLUB CHAIRS, ARMCHAIRS, & WING CHAIRS

No matter where you go in the world, sexy, overstuffed, well-made chairs are always the first items to go at flea markets (particularly in Paris as Americans compete to snatch them up). Especially the kind that let you curl up in it or swing your leg over the side when you're lost in a good book. If you find a cozy *leather* one with a worn patina and great springs, you've found the ring in the Cracker Jack box. (In the South, old mohair armchairs are also considered a find because they can be easily slipcovered.)

Note: While sensual worn leather is the ultimate find, the current thirst for armchairs seems to be making *all* of them look great. If quality is your primary objective though, you may want to hold out for a hardwood frame and hand-tied coil springs.

COCKTAIL SHAKERS

Shaken—not stirred. Modernistic sterling silver, silver plate, aluminum, and glass cocktail shakers were created in an incredible variety of designs from geometric to Deco and shapes from zeppelins to golf bags.

All of them recall a time when urbane "moderns" toasted the sparkling future ahead—especially during prohibition. The glittering prizes of these machine-age classics are from influential manufacturers like Reed & Barton, International Silver Co., Revere Copper and Brass Co., and Chase Brass and Copper Co. If you're feeling lucky, search for Art Deco cocktail shakers designed by industrial designers like Norman Bel Geddes and Lurelle Guild.

COMMEMORATIVE MEDALS

Bronze, brass, maybe even gold medallions were cast to commemorate all kinds of things from sporting events to weddings and historical events. They're an affordable, evocative form of "small sculpture" that are available internationally. And they're a great gift if you find one that suits an upcoming event. If a dealer carries commemorative medals, they're usually in the case next to war medals and pins.

COLE SLAW BOARDS

Carved wood cutting boards from the turn of the century with hand-wrought metal fittings boast great authenticity and great style. The metal fittings were used for grating and the wood for chopping, but these days they look wonderful hanging on the wall in a dining room or a kitchen.

COPKO & DANSK COOKWARE

So well designed. So stylish. So '60s. Nature meets metal, enamel cast iron tea kettle and cook pan classics pulse with color. Orange. Yellow. Bright Blue. If you find one, examine it carefully—enamel cast iron has a tendency to chip.

DEPRESSION GLASS

Depression glass is the generic name for a huge category of mass-produced clear and colored glass and dinnerware manufactured from 1925 through the 1940s by a great many companies. It's not just an all-American staple in high- and low-end markets across the country—its vast permutations make it a lesson in American history as well. There are a remarkable number of patterns and colors available to choose from. (It was even made into utility wares like canisters, icebox dishes, and lemon reamers.)

These days the killer pattern is clear glass Manhattan, made by Anchor Hocking between 1938 and 1941. Look for the cocktail glasses.

However, trends come and go. And Manhattan is only one of hundreds of patterns that come under the heading of Depression glass. You'll have to decide between etched designs like Adam or Cherry Blossom or raised designs with fruit and flower patterns such as Open Rose and Sharon.

And it only gets more complicated—there are Hobnail and Ribbon wares, cubist designs molded into rectangular and diamond patterns, Art Deco–influenced geometric designs like Imperial Octagon and U.S. Octagon—even glass designed to look like cut glass from the nineteenth century in patterns with names like Floral and Diamond Band. Plus there are enameled and silk-screened patterns developed during the 1940s and star patterns like Miss America, Cameo, and Hockin's Miss America.

With the exception of really well-known classics, there are so many patterns available from so many manufacturers, and so much overlap, that even the exact name to use for a pattern may be in doubt. Much doubt.

If not by pattern, you can also collect by color including ruby, cobalt, and green solid-color sets. Before you get started, keep in mind that over the last decade Depression glass has managed to become so popular it's become expensive—and its number of admirers continues to grow. Be alert, no matter what the pattern, design, or colors you decide to collect. Reproductions are a problem that is destined to get worse. You've got to see a lot of original Depression glass to recognize the true colors on sight and to observe what patterns of daily wear looked like. Nobody saved this once cheap glass for their Sunday best in its day. Reproduction patterns are too sharp, without realistic signs of daily use, and the colors tend to look muddy compared to the originals.

What Makes a House a Home?

"A tape measure."

—Anne Groer, *Washington Post* gossip columnist

her collections:

Art Deco Chinese rugs
Poodle jewelry
Peculiar handbags
Turquoise kitchen appliances and housewares
Vintage hankies and aprons
Trench art (particularly World War I)
Gilbert Rhode furniture
Political wristwatches
Taxidermy
1939 World's Fair flatware
Lusterware hot chocolate and tea services

$E = mc^2$

Hard to imagine this as we approach the end of the millennium, but at the beginning of this century, a physicist was once a reigning celebrity.

In fact, Albert Einstein was actually so popular in the early 1900s that he was frequently asked for autographs by all kinds of people. And as a man who invariably went the extra mile, Einstein didn't just sign his name on cocktail napkins for fans—he also added his famous formula.

Surprisingly, or maybe not so surprisingly, these many cocktail napkins or autograph book pages frequently surface on Internet flea site auctions.

EARLY ELECTRONICS AS ART

Bakelite radios, transistor radios, record players, historic Apple computers—don't think of them as the dinosaur age of audio-electronics or computers—think of these early electronics as collectibles with shapely nostalgic lines. If you're planning to actually use your vintage TV set, keep in mind that pre-1949 sets only get thirteen stations, max!

Transistor radios are so plentiful that collectors actually specialize by design, by whether the manufacturer is American or Japanese, as well as by subcategories like integrated circuit boards.

ELECTRIC FANS

Graham Greene might have favored the overhead variety, but desktop rubber-bladed electric fans from the early '40s reek of chic. Vintage Vortexes had metal blades but they aren't bad either—their retro silhouette is combined with an engine straight out of the 1940s aircraft industry. They even come in a color known as Lambert green, a.k.a. olive. Early Westinghouse models came in Art Deco designs.

Expect to pay anywhere from $50 to $400 for one of these cool beauties depending on the design and whether the fan has been rewired or is merely decorative. Many fans were manufactured in St. Louis, so if you're ever in Missouri, hit the flea markets and antique malls.

ESTATE JEWELRY

Estate jewelry is now so popular it's even sold in some department stores. For style and workmanship, estate jewelry is inherently valuable. There are numerous books on it—but the general rule of thumb is that when you begin buying estate jewelry you look at the front. As you develop expertise in the genre you'll begin to look at the back of a brooch just as carefully. Evaluate the quality of how it was made initially—and then see how it was treated in its lifetime by flipping it over. Was it repaired? Were stones exchanged? You may also want to ask the dealer to write a return policy so you can have your estate jewelry independently appraised.

FIESTA

Never-say-die durable, these color-drenched dinnerware classics were the most popular pottery of the 1930s. They were manufactured by the Homer Laughlin China Company from the 1930s until the early 1970s. Some say their popularity has peaked. Others disagree.

If Fiesta is your addiction, you should know that some pieces are far more valuable than others. Form and color are the defining moments of the genre. (The original five colors: red, dark blue, chartreuse, brilliant yellow, and ivory are the most valuable.)

Dinnerware is only part of the famous Fiesta bounty. Interesting side pieces you may want to investigate include relish trays, bud vases, carafes, egg cups, juicers, and marmalade jars.

Fiesta has also been reissued recently. Some people even prefer the new collection given that its glaze is made without uranium.

Think Karen Silkwood

Before you buy glazed crockery produced prior to 1972, you should know that early orange and red glazes contain enough uranium to register on a Geiger counter—and experts in reglazing are rare. If you've spent the time and money it takes these days to collect an entire dinner set of Fiesta ware, chances are good you won't be using it to eat on every night.

FIFTIES CERAMICS

Decorators once called these "accents"; they were more like decorative accents with attitude. Parisian poodles. Chartreuse panthers. Dancing horses. Amoeba-shaped abstracts. Optimism radiates from atomic age ceramics. They look best with curvy '50s kidney tables, vintage print pillows or curtains, and the classic '50s color scheme: black, gold, pink, and turquoise.

FIFTIES & SIXTIES ITALIAN
& SCANDINAVIAN GLASS

Great imported glass pieces are a find. The first time you see any of these fantastic plates, vases, and bowls, you'll know you've found something special and colorful. Especially when you see case glass pieces—which were made by fusing transparent with opaque glass.

✳ *Blenko* These big, gorgeous, handblown, simplistic shapes came in bright resonant colors from the Blenko factory in West Virginia. In 1959 and 1960, Blenko etched a sandblasted stamp on the bottom, which included its name and the hand logo.

☆ *Venini* Suddenly, postwar Italian glass from the Venini factory on the island of Murano in Italy is everywhere. The pieces pulse with primary hues, gorgeous shapes, and sometimes combine transparent with opaque glass, or are banded with crinoline ribbons of glass. Better yet, both the low-end and the high-end Venini are eminently desirable. Bright, bold '60s glass from Italy by Tobia Scarpa, Thomas Stearns, Checco Ongarro, Tapio Wirkkala, and Toots Zynasky are especially hot.

♣ *Scandinavian glass* from the '50s, '60s, and '70s was blown into gorgeous, compelling colors and shapes and is every bit as remarkable as Italian glass—and sometimes slightly less expensive.

Art glass is more valuable if the original sticker is still on it. This is because many of the original owners tended to place a higher premium on the name of the store they bought the glass from than the manufacturer/designer of the glass. So don't be surprised if a Blenko you stumble on at a tag sale is described as Neiman Marcus or Gump's glass.

FISHING PARAPHERNALIA

Split bamboo fly rods made by master craftsmen are quite a catch. So are fishing tackle baskets, ice fishing gear, creels, antique flies, decoys, and mounted taxidermy fish.

The older and more used the piscatorial paraphernalia, the better the find.

If you're in the market for true antiques, remember that reels with maker's marks are always more valuable than those without. And if you've got a mantelpiece that could use a mounted fish, hold out for a trophy catch in a bow-fronted case with a descriptive label.

Look for shape, texture, and the patina of use and authenticity if you're buying mounted fish for decoration. Hang them, frame them, or add small specimens to a *wunderkammer* (a table of wonders) curio cabinet. (Or mix them with other sporting goods to cover an entire wall.)

FLOW BLUE

Before glaze was perfected, blue prints made at numerous potters in Staffordshire used to bleed and smudge. Even the marks on the back of the plates often bled so badly that they were useless for identification. Yet in a quirk of fate, these messy blue and white plates are now considered quite the blue plate special—particularly in the South. And if the bleed was so bad that the entire design is completely unrecognizable, well, that's as perfect as it gets!

FOUNTAIN PENS

Form plus function are what make early twentieth-century fountain pens increasingly popular. Look for wonderful American brands like Waterman, Parker, Sheaffer, Wahl-Eversharp, and Conklin or distinctive foreign pens by foreign manufacturers like Mont Blanc and Pelikan. The more unusual the more valuable.

If you've already found the ultimate fountain pen, or even the perfect pen and pencil set, keep your eye out for the penultimate inkwell. You'll find them in brass, cast iron, cut glass, porcelain, or cast metal with glass inserts.

GAME BOARDS

These days old game boards have legs. They're showing up in more and more homes and offices as art. The type fonts are usually one-of-a-kind, and their attractions can range from childhood nostalgia to folk art in action. Current collector favorites include Magilla Gorilla, Restless Gun, Voyage to the Bottom of the Sea, and of course, *Gunsmoke.*

But before you snap up any game to display as art, make sure it's not suffering from the kind of sun damage that comes with sitting outdoors at a dusty market weekend after weekend or scotch tape repairs and old-fashioned dirt. And, if your intentions are to actually use it as a game—and not as art—make sure it still has the original instructions and all its pieces.

GARDEN FURNITURE

Spotting old outdoor furniture, especially the cast-iron, wrought-iron, and cast-marble and -stone variety has become a weekend sport in itself. Even vintage redwood picnic tables have become quite a weekend coup. Late '50s whimsical wire side chairs, pedestal-based chaise lounges, and low tables are well worth a field trip any time.

On the East Coast, you'll find many tightly woven wire mesh sculptural armchairs by Russell Woodward (as well as his capsule-shaped sofas and chairs of woven fiber with wrought-iron legs).

On the West Coast stay on the lookout for stylish tubular aluminum outdoor furniture wrapped with bright vinyl straps. Produced by the Brown Jordan company from the 1940s through the 1960s, its look is timeless.

Demand for old stone garden statuary and benches is now so strong throughout the South that stoneware is actually being stolen from cemeteries and front yards. Many local garden fans have resorted to bringing their smaller pieces indoors!

But no matter what part of the country you live in, any time you snare a cast-stone birdbath, urn, or garden bench, it's a bonanza. Ditto for cast-iron fountains, garden gates, and love seats.

Note: Chipped or peeled paint and rusted metal is the first choice of many decorators.

GARDEN PLANTERS

Look for moss-eaten clay pots, oversized terra-cotta pots, window boxes, Stangel flowerpots, watering pots, and cast-stone planters. The older and more weathered the better. (Actually you can even make relatively recent stone planters look really old by coating them with yogurt and leaving them until morning. You'll be genuinely thrilled at how many years of green crud you can create in one night.)

GARDEN TOOLS

Garden tools are utilitarian chic at its handiest—especially tools with painted or unpainted wood handles and distressed metalwork. From old trowels to rakes and hoes, used garden tools are now objects of beauty—and integrity.

If you're collecting them as casual art, only you will know what you are looking for in the way of patina and authenticity. If you plan to actually use a tool, make sure the metal isn't too rusted or corroded, but don't forget that a lot of old metal can be cleaned up with a bit of steel wool.

GOLF COLLECTIBLES

Off we go into the wild green yonder. Not just a subcategory of sports, golf collectibles have carved out their own turf. Favorites include early Burke irons with wood shafts, Spalding steel shaft putters, '60s leather golf bags, leather score card cases, Art Deco golfer radiator caps, early U.S. Open paperweights, and yellow dot Chemico Bob golf balls. Even old golf books have made the cut.

"GUESS WHERE WE WENT?"

There was a time when family vacations involved driving for days and collecting decals when you got somewhere. Look for decals of national parks, states, flowers, and semi-clad women. Or collect gas station patches, Boy Scout patches, National Park patches, or firehouse patches. Frame them or sew them on to hooded sweatshirts, baseball caps, bathrobes, or pillowcases.

HEYWOOD-WAKEFIELD

Spare, streamlined, and blond. Sleek, natural wood Heywood-Wakefield mid-century tables and chairs and sets were origi-nally intended to become a "design for the masses." Given its current popularity, this sleek '50s furniture line seems to have achieved its goal and then some.

Tip: Before World War II, Heywood-Wakefield was made from maple. But after the war, its pieces were made from birch.

IMMIGRANT TRUNKS

Norwegian and Scandinavian farmers en route to the Midwest once sent all their goods to places like Minnesota and Iowa in heavy pine trunks with metal corner fittings and their addresses carefully painted on the sides. Once they arrived safely in the Midwest, these trunks became storage chests. Today they still store memories as well as an almost black fin-ish from almost a century of use.

INFANT OF PRAGUE

Build your own grotto with mammoth religious statues, tile floors, mirrors, larger-than-life rosary beads—and most importantly—bleeding, crying saints. The bigger the better. Don't overlook vintage Santo de Palo figures, the carved household saints from Puerto Rico. Carved from wood, their painted surfaces age in wonderful ways. Or find yourself moved by the simplicity of "ex votos": small devotional paintings on rusting tin that petition or thank saints.

What Makes a House a Home?

"Choosing things with emotional resonance."

—Mary Evans, literary agent

her collections:

Oddfellows memorabilia
Utopian socialist furniture
Mulberry ironstone china
Mulberry polychrome china
Great Lakes fishing lure
Gilt valances
Cast-iron animals and figures
Wooden and ivory dice
Pressed glass glassware
Painted wood grain furniture

JADE-ITE

This Fire-King 1940s Depression-glass restaurant ware was made by a company called Anchor Hocking Glass Corporation. It was sold in sets in the 1940s through the 1970s in vast quantities. And while it may be called Jade-ite, this opaque light green colored glass oddly enough looks more like sea foam or celery than jade. (The occasional ridged pattern is called Jane-Ray.)

Originally produced for restaurants, Jade-ite comes in every shape, dish, and side dish imaginable. Round plates. Oval plates. Platter plates. Soup bowls. Cereal bowls. Sugar bowls. Salt and pepper shakers.

KITCHEN PARAPHERNALIA

Mid-century kitchen goods have an awesome following. They personify not just great design and simplicity but an emotional thirst for a simpler time when loving came from the oven—not the microwave.

In addition, most vintage kitchen goods were made with durable metals, which makes them inherently more valuable. Look for cast iron, stainless steel, and nickel plate. The well-constructed metal motors of some of the old ice crushers, blenders, and the like continue to outlast many of their modern counterparts.

If you need a mid-century shopping list, consider these nostalgia necessities: Pyrex and ceramic batter bowls, industrial design lemon squeezers, ceramic cookie jars, measuring cups, Mix Masters, streamlined toasters, handblown Chemex drip pots, Osterizers, Bakelite-handled flatware, spun aluminum Thermoses, carafes, souvenir salt and pepper shakers, old canisters (especially French ones), Russel Wright kitchen anything, electric percolators, juice glasses, lazy Susans, cast-iron frying pans and corn bread molds, stainless steel ladles, and cutting boards. Flea markets are also a great source of unusual kitchen appliances like raisin seeders, apple parers, potato mashers, and ice cream scoops.

Kitchen tools like spatulas, cakes servers, ladles, and whisks designed by industrial designer Henry Dreyfuss for the Washburn Company now appear at every pier show across the country. Never overlook Ekco Products Flint kitchen tools either—they've held up as classics since they were first designed by committee in the 1940s.

Tip: If you are buying extravagantly streamlined toasters, blenders, or any other mechanical appliance that you intend to use, make sure the design doesn't get in the way. While some early appliance designs have ended up in the Museum of Modern Art, others can burn toast to a crisp.

LINENS

Vintage mint-condition linens add romantic oomph to all kinds of bedrooms, dining rooms, guest rooms, and nurseries.

Think damask, cotton, and lace tablecloths, commemorative tea towels, bridge sets, baby bibs, and kitchen towels stitched from pre-stamped embroidery kits in the early twentieth century. Draperies, samplers, throws, small pieces like hand-stitched bibs, and towels even look interesting matted and framed. Look carefully for signs of wear, patching, or stains before you buy.

Bed linens are equally compelling. Think satin duvets, embroidered trousseau pillowcases, hotel linens, and cruise linens. Railroad linens are particularly popular; their white-on-white embroidery radiates luxury. You'll find the corporate name—usually Fred Harvey—woven into the border of the fabric. (Harvey once owned all the railroads.)

LOW-END INDUSTRIAL DESIGNERS

Now and then you see a 1950s or 1960s barber chair, dentist chair, conference table, or office end table from God knows where that is old, amazing, and of unknown parentage. It could be blond, metal, or a mix of both, as long as it has a low-key attitude all its own.

This mid-century bounty includes industrial-strength classic armchairs, wool-tweed sofas, conference tables, platform benches, ceramic clocks, kitchenware, restaurant furnishings, silverware, airline goods, beauty salon furnishings, and hotel interiors.

Tip: If your end goal is urban eclecticism—you should know that low-end industrial designs, for reasons too strange to analyze, invariably look great mixed in with African tribal art collections.

MAJOR KITCHEN APPLIANCES

In some circles, a Viking stove is every bit as valuable as an Eames chair or a Stickley table, while mid-century modern refrigerators, with their clean rounded lines and memorable colors, are developing a reputation for being so cool they are urban chic. It helps if you don't mind a small freezer compartment and resurrecting the ritual of defrosting the refrigerator.

Any time you spot a red-hot stove like the Magic Chef from the 1930s or an old restaurant Viking stove, you are looking at a miracle find—especially if you need a range with more than one oven and up to eight burners. Compared to modern ovens, these super stoves are singularly stylish workhorses built for the duration. (Just don't expect oven lights, pilotless ignition, or sealed burners in a gas stove.) Plus, if you're buying a former restaurant stove, make sure you're not buying the kind that needs a restaurant-caliber ventilation system as well.

Unless you're buying a fully restored stove or refrigerator, be certain you actually know contractors who can help you refurbish, revamp, or even repaint vintage refrigerators and stoves.

Investigate clubs like The Old Appliance Club, c/o JES Enterprises, PO Box 65, Ventura, CA 93002. E-mail address jes@wes.net. They publish four newsletters a year with information, repair advice, and "for sale" and "wanted to buy" classifieds. As a club member you will also be entitled to free consultation on repairs or repair source referrals. Dues are $18 annually. They also have a free pamphlet you can request called "Keepers vs. Clunkers."

MAMMY WARE

Aunt Jemima salt and pepper shakers, jockey garden statuary, and all kinds of other stereotypical references from America's racial history are being avidly collected by African-Americans these days. Context is everything.

MAPS AND GLOBES

Easy to rationalize—your children will learn how to find New Zealand without using a computer—old globes and maps are modern talismans for the global village.

Choose from illuminated globes, gesso globes, biscuit tin globes, inflatable globes, AM radio globes, and steel globes. Bigger is better. Don't just settle for pale blue oceans either—the great ones have deep blue seas or even black backgrounds. There are numerous globes around so you should always hold out for excellent metal or wood hardware and glorious colors. Make sure there is no fading or discoloration.

Even more dazzling are armillary spheres that demonstrate the movement of the planets in the solar system.

McCOBB

If you're looking for furniture at flea markets or boutiques, chances are you'll come across this 1950s mass-produced modular furniture made of birch and maple. The more upscale McCobb collection from the Directional Group used walnut and brass. This may be why this shapely Scandinavian-inspired furniture is en route to becoming a classic must-have once again as we approach the millennium. Look for tables, modular wall units, bureaus, credenzas, and more.

Tip: Unless it has fallen off, mint quality McCobb pieces should have a label or plaque inside a drawer.

MEDICAL ILLUSTRATIONS

Anatomy is destiny deluxe. Early black-and-white hand-drawn medical illustrations of anatomy can be quite beautiful—even mysterious—when they're matted and framed. Best of all, while the entire genre of medical nostalgia is on the rise, medical illustrations are still undervalued. Even some of the oversized hanging anatomy charts developed for classrooms can be graphically compelling when seen in a new context, like your home.

MERCURY GLASS

Great round ornamental balls of "silver" from the nineteenth century are shining brighter than ever! Made from double-walled handblown glass that has been given an exterior coat of silver and then vacuum sealed, they have a futuristic sheen and shape that looks spectacular anywhere. Look for mercury glass globes at estate sales, pier shows, or at the Paris flea market. They don't make mercury like that anymore.

METAL FURNITURE

Austere gray metal mixes exceptionally well with other twentieth century styles. After all, metal is a natural material. Once it has been oxidized or stripped down and sealed, all kinds of streamlined metal tables and chairs can resemble stripped-down French Futuristic furniture—which is the chicest of all metal finds.

Look for low-end industrial design tables, benches, cabinets, occasional chairs, bookcases from factories, hospitals, doctors offices, and offices in general. Even hotel liquidations can turn up versatile metal serving tables. And keep your eyes open to the possibilities. If the lines are great, it may be worthwhile to look closely at painted and fake wood grain metal pieces—if you think you can find someone to strip and coat your find with anti-rust lacquer. Or, if you don't blanch at high-end prices, seek out American industrial design giant Warren McArthur's tubular metal furniture designs.

MID-CENTURY MODERN FURNITURE

Call it Organic Modernism, International Modernism, post-War Optimism, or post-American Streamlined Moderne, but whatever you do, don't overlook these classics at a yard sale, auction warehouse, or second-hand office furniture store.

The top line of the chic is *anything* by Warren McArthur, Charles Eames, George Nelson, and Isamu Noguchi, as well as '50s and '60s modern classic furniture designed for the Knoll Group by designers like Harry Bertoia, Alvar Aalto, and Eero Saarinen.

Not only has each of these designers' confident, free-form designs survived long beyond their fifteen-minute allotment, but their diversity is truly phenomenal. Influenced by molecular structures, rational thinking, and the abstract forms of Surrealist painters, these designers changed the language of decorative art in solution-led, functional, and even brash ways.

There is a lot of mid-century furniture to choose from. Mid-century designers were so prolific you'll find their designs mixed in with home furnishings, office furniture, glass design, and kitchenware sale lots at hotel sales, public auctions, and flea markets. If you're truly, wildly lucky, you'll find a piece at a yard sale run by a clueless grandchild. Otherwise, scope out their work at modernism shows, pier shows, and auction houses across the country.

MOROCCAN MELLOW

Voluptuous Middle-Eastern accessories have a way of turning up in curious places like flea markets, pier shows, and junk stores.

Look for mosaic-topped and carved wood tables, scrolled ironwork screens, lavishly etched low brass-tray coffee tables, provincial earthenware, temple lanterns, Byzantine fabric throw pillows, and Arabian-patterned embroidered linens. Whether you've unearthed a damascened steel sword or a Turkish watercolor brought back from a souk, Middle-Eastern finds offer a decorative, exotic, mystical charm that feels curiously hip as we approach a new millennium.

MOUNTED BONES

Think of them bones as lodgeware. Bring home mounted antlers, dinosaur bones, coyote and cow skulls, or examples of Adirondack and Western art. Or just collect bones for their bleached colors and natural shapes. While you're at it, dig around for arrowheads, especially framed collections. If you are an enthusiast, don't overlook the Jackson Hole, Wyoming, Boy Scout Bone Jamboree. It's a great source for antlers.

Tip: Some people swear that nothing brings out the oyster color of the average computer shell like a really old but small coyote skull resting on top.

MUSICAL INSTRUMENTS

Big and brassy, sleek and silver, or classic mellow wooden musical instruments are always magical. Flea markets may not be the place to find perfectly tuned instruments, but they do turn up some singularly atmospheric finds. A silver flute. An old bass. A well used set of calypso drums. A tambourine. It doesn't have to be a classic Steinway to add new dimensions to any decor. If flea markets don't turn up the tuba of your dreams, try a pawn shop.

What Makes a House a Home?

"Your pillow."

—Barbara Glauber, graphic designer

her collections:

- Antique potato mashers
- Old game boards that feature maps
- Postcards promoting states
- Pens with things floating in them

NATIVE AMERICAN ART

Deep history with extraordinary aesthetic appeal. These days, the hunt is on for twentieth-century examples of Navajo blankets, Zuni jars, woven baskets, Eskimo finger masks, quill work, and beaded clothing. Things turn up in Alaska, the Northwest Coast, the Plains, and the Southwest.

Tip: Dust any basket made of pine needles, straw or grass with a sable artist's brush to clean it; don't use water!

NATURAL OBJECTS

Commission Mother Nature as an artist. Tumble weeds. Weathered gourds. Bird's nests. Exceptional shells. Glass floats that wash up on shore. Vintage small animal skulls and bones, or possibly a full-size dinosaur bone. The natural world is waiting to be found. Look for weathered authenticity, evocative shapes, and calming colors.

OCEAN LINER LUXURIES

The *Normandie*. The Cunard steamship. The S.S. *Paris*. Invariably—whether the insignia is from America, England, Germany, or France—loot from the high seas looks stylish. The list of seaworthy collectibles includes transoceanic liners, steamers, and clipper ships.

Look for model boats, insignia-emblazoned sugar bowls and creamers, illustrious stock certificates, detailed deck plans, tin signs, life preservers, promotional posters, pins, tin cups, and more.

ODDFELLOW OBJECTS

Oddfellows was a nineteenth-century secret society with lodges across the country. They believed in freedom for all humankind. They built orphanages, initiated pensions for widows, and left a legacy of carved ceremonial objects based on symbolism of time passing—and the Bible.

Mystery and pageantry still resonate in their plaques, spears, and utilitarian objects.

OFFICE INDUSTRIAL

Odds are you spend more time in your office than your home. So why not humanize pervasive '90s technology with desks, drafting tables, conference tables, or file cabinets from the mid–twentieth century industrial designers like Warren McArthur, Charles Eames, Paul McCobb, George Nelson, and Terrance Harold Robsjohn Gibbings.

Coordinate or contrast your office industrial finds with vintage desk sets, clocks, pen trays, book ends, ink wells, magnifying glasses, or chromium staplers, hole punchers, paper clip holders, and vintage paper cutters that were made any time from the late 1800s to the 1950s.

But don't stop there. Round out your retro-office decor collection with zany office supplies and ephemera from the typewriter decades like liquid white-out, white-out tape by the yard, and even typewriter ribbon tins.

OLD STRAINERS AND COLANDERS

Look for colanders with interesting feet and amusing designs. The old ones came with stars, dots, and stripes. Of course, you can always use them as strainers, but they can be equally functional as centerpieces, fruit bowls, or even lampshade sconces.

OUIJI BOARDS

Let the dubious call them game boards. Vintage ouiji boards are an early look into the future, carved from wood and complete with fascinating typefaces and great graphics.

What Makes a House a Home?

"The Mana (spirit)."

—Janu Cassidy, owner of Radio Hula

her collections:

S.S. *Hawaii* spoons
Hula doll knodders
Hula girl postcards
Hawaiian wooden perfume bottles

PAINT-BY-NUMBER ART

Paint-by-number kits were astoundingly popular in their day. They range from dog pictures to knockoffs of the Great Masters. Look for the ones that were lovingly and precisely executed right down to the frames—especially the burned wood ones. Match your decor with a quasi-original Rembrandt, horse portrait, naive portrait, or bucolic splendor. Paint-by-number art is fun, still cheap, and looks great in a guest bathroom.

PAPER DOLLS

Search out 1950s stars from the sunshine years like Gale Storm, the Lennon Sisters, or Sonja Henie. Katy Keene would also be fun. These are hard to find, but the fashion tips alone make retro paper dolls cutting edge.

Tip: They also look great framed and hung in a closet.

PICNIC SETS

Why lug a brand new Kmart cooler to the beach when you can carry a cool vintage Scotch plaid cooler instead? These classic plastic totes wipe clean with a sponge and look great on the beach.

If plastic doesn't work with the champagne and pâté menu you had in mind, look for a vintage wicker picnic set with great accoutrements like tiny salt and pepper shakers, utensils, and covered dishes.

PICTURE FRAMES

These are always the first goods to go at any upscale tag sale, yard sale, or flea market. Don't worry about what's in them. Look for gold leaf, metal work, or Della Robbia (the Italian carved fruit and flowers technique). Don't just look at the paint on the front when you examine a vintage wooden picture frame, study the back of the frame as well. The unpainted wood may be far more interesting than the front.

Don't worry about bad glass or stained matting. You can have them replaced easily.

Once you start looking, you'll find picture frames everywhere. So whenever you're at a church sale, a flea market, or an auction warehouse, always take a minute to study the frames. Even if the frame itself is no great shakes, don't be deterred. If the dimensions work for you, envision it on a wall with ten or more other frames all painted the same color, like Navaho white.

POKER CHIPS

Computer chips aren't the only game in town. Vintage poker chips are hot stuff from Atlantic City to Las Vegas to London. Limited edition chips, like those given out on New Year's Eve at fabled gambling places or those emblazoned with sports figures have become so popular over the last decade that they now command Websites, a magazine, and special shows held in convention halls at—you guessed it—gambling casinos!

POPCORN POPPERS

These may not seem like aliens-have-landed, futuristic sculptures until you see one! The great ones are the early electric models made in the early 1930s through the 1940s to look as if they could take off for another solar system. They were made from aluminum or steel and came with painted wood or walnut handles and domed glass tops—all the better to see the action. Plus, all these early wonders were designed with raised feet so they could stand dramatically on the kitchen counter as they popped.

PSYCHO CERAMICS

These three-dimensional strange blob figures were popular in the '60s and widely distributed on the West Coast—which is where you are most likely to find them to this very day. They visually depict the word "psycho" and if these creepy six-inch statues produced by the Kreiss company aren't creepy enough for the likes of you, then bring home the matching mugs and ashtrays.

Or consider subcategories in the genre. The Kreiss company is equally well-known for their line of Beatnik men and women characters decorated with Daddy-O cool sayings. (For some unknown reason, the women characters are especially hard to find.) That's not all. The Kreiss Company has also produced a line of memorable ceramic alter-ego characters, which were equally bizarre in curious ways all their own. One example is the screaming bald-headed woman with attached children.

RED WING POTTERY

Industrial design stars like Eva Zeisel worked for Red Wing in the 1940s. Which may explain why this Midwest pottery was known for its artisan details and free-flowing lines. Red Wing was often hand painted, so each piece had a slightly different design. The most popular of Red Wing's "detergent proof, oven proof" dinnerware patterns have wonderfully evocative names like Bobwhite, Pompeii, Lute Song, and Lotus. If you're not in need of a dinner set, not to worry; Red Wing Pottery also made crocks, beehive jugs, water coolers, and many commemorative pieces.

RING-DING

These graphic Depression glass juice glasses and pitchers were once ubiquitous and memorable thanks to the red, yellow, green, orange, and white rings around the exterior top half of the clear ridged glass. In fact the pattern was so popular it even came in cocktail shaker and shot glass renditions. Now that colorful interiors are becoming more and more popular, Ring-Ding has surfaced once again as a must-have.

Tip: You'll get a much better price if you find the glasses or a pitcher sold separately than as a set.

ROBOTS AND ROCKETS

After Frankenstein—but long before anybody had ever seen Blade Runner, or even dreamed of having a computer in their own home—rockets and robots reigned supreme as the future of the future.

The reminders of that nostalgic Buck Rogers vision are these 1950s mechanical tin talismans (friction, wind-up, and battery operated) and illustrations. Mysteriously enough, old robots are hard to find, but if you're in a must-have mode, make do with early '80s *Star Wars* clones R2-D2 and, of course, C-3PO. Or tune in mega-cool yellow robot radios from the '60s. However if you manage to stumble across any of the Japanese six to eight–inch tall robots made after the war from discarded Heinz 57 tin cans, you have entered the planet of luck. If, by some chance, you discover any fifteen-inch robots made for Matsudaya in the 1950s like Machine Man, Sonic Robot, Giant Sonic Robot, or Lavender Robot, call Sotheby's immediately or build a small shrine for it—it is worth many thousands of dollars.

Even without the good looks of a robot or the streamlined physique of rockets, alien collectibles are gaining steam in this genre. Look for *E.T.* action figures, *Planet of the Apes* game boards, or *Battlestar Galactica* Cylon helmet radios.

Caution: If you are on the trail of robot, rocket, or alien transport model kits like the Invisible Flying Saucer, be careful of open boxes—missing pieces could give your brain a meltdown.

SCIENTIFIC SPECIMENS

Modern talismans can take the form of old mahogany and brass telescopes, microscopes, compasses, apothecary jars, sextants (the instruments used to measure nautical distance), and architectural tools. Think of them as sculpture, as personal totems, or as graphic reminders of the mind-bending accomplishments that took place long before the first mainframe was ever plugged in.

SLAT FURNITURE

Old wooden slat furniture resonates with relaxed authenticity. Think well-used L.L. Bean, Adirondack, and campaign style in library tables, end tables, or cruise chairs. But best of all, old wooden slat furniture mixes with just about anything mid-century.

SMILEY FACE STUFF

In the late 1960s and early 1970s, big yellow smiley reigned as an icon long before Microsoft launched Bob. If big smiley works for you, look for the mood man on cookie jars, juice glasses, kitchen lights, lamp shades, lunch boxes, T-shirts, and who knows what else. It was a strange time.

SPORTS PARAPHERNALIA

Snowshoes, old catcher's masks, batting helmets, Spalding wood baseball bats (watch out for splinters), vintage tennis rackets, Flexible Flyer wooden sleds, 1930s football helmets, vintage skis, Indian clubs, and even old roller skates can look wonderful hanging on a wall.

Collect them because you're a sports fiend or because you see them as art. The more action they've seen, the more they hold their own as a powerfully evocative vintage object with wonderful authenticity, natural color pallette, great shapes, and uniquely tactile textures.

SPRATLING SILVER

William Spratling's clean-lined sterling silver jewelry, hollow ware, and belt buckles were collected by the likes of Errol Flynn, Leon Trotsky, and Bette Davis. Best of all, his celebrated silver jewelry turns up regularly at flea markets and antique shows across the country.

You'll have to learn to recognize at least sixteen marks for this remarkably prolific silversmith if you're looking for pre-1967 (the year he died) designs. Spratling's factory in Taxco, Mexico, is still going strong producing this casually compelling silver. (Another six marks distinguish the post–1967 items, which are carried by many prominent department stores and boutiques.) In addition to his unique non-representational forms, Spratling pieces incorporate astrological symbols, lizards, jaguars, hummingbirds, leaves, shells, and Jazz Age motifs.

Mint Conditions

Always insist on great stuff.

Do a little soul searching before you decide to buy anything; these days we've all got too much stuff. Try not to snap up name brands just because they are part of a popular movement—no matter how trendy the name.

For example, McCoy Pottery is popular, but it is not always great pottery. Some of it is little more than kitsch. Luckily, there's so much of it to choose from that there is no reason not to hold out for great pieces. In other words. don't buy a frog design McCoy pot just because the price is great. But if you have an unconscious affinity for frogs, you don't care who made it, and it's practically free—that's a different story.

There is so much spectacular stuff out there from so many designers and from so many decades that you really don't have to settle for second best. There is no real reason to buy chipped pieces, colors that aren't rich, or fabric that is stained. Sooner or later, you'll find the same piece in "mint condition" and regret the one with the stain, the crack, or the missing piece. Which is why you should examine anything you buy very carefully. Think like a professional before you let your adrenaline get in the way. Ask yourself questions such as: "Is the finish glowing?" "If repairs have been made, are they of high quality?" "Are all the accessories included and intact?" For example, if you're considering a vintage picnic basket, does it have all of its original serving containers?

If the answer to all of the above questions is yes, then the basket would probably be judged to be in fine condition. If, say, the exterior wicker of this picnic basket is perfect, but the basket is missing one of the dinner forks, then it's in good condition—and shouldn't cost you as much as if it were perfect. If several of the accessories are missing, some of its exterior wicker is unraveling, and the inside cloth is stained, depending on the extent of the damage, a professional would consider it to be in average or poor condition. In that case, it should be very inexpensive. You should probably think seriously before making the purchase—unless you genuinely love a serious flaw for personal reasons.

But while finish is important and having all of the working pieces is quite a big deal, these aren't the only speed bumps in determining value—especially if it is an expensive purchase. Authenticity is an issue of increasing importance. If a dealer claims a desk is fifty years old, look inside and at the back of the drawers. Do they look like they have been in use for fifty years?

Are the proportions and the weight correct? Is there anything about it that doesn't ring true—including the price?

For example, if you're considering an Arts and Crafts piece, examine the finish and check to see if any repairs have been made, if anything is missing, and if the proportions look correct. (Neither the height, width, or the depth should overwhelm the piece.) All the details are critical. Hardware should be heavy and hammered, not lightweight and stamped. Small panes of glass in a bookcase are more valuable than large panes. In other words, not all Arts and Crafts furniture is equal—but the more you know, the better your ability to judge.

Another example is tortoiseshell objects. Real tortoiseshell is not only expensive, but it's rarely in perfect condition. So if you see a piece that doesn't exhibit even the slightest hint of minor damage or small repairs after years of alleged use then it's probably not real tortoise. (In fact, it could be made of lexane or some other hard plastic that resists denting, burning, or scraping—which could be nice too if you think about it, it's just not tortoise.)

Evaluating the authenticity of true antiques is complicated. Many people even use appraisers to scout auctions ahead of time. The alter-economy is far less demanding, though, as long as you only buy what you love.

STAINLESS STEEL CUTLERY

Stainless steel was introduced and accepted by the consumer market in the 1950s thanks to its exceptional free-flowing organic design. It hasn't been quite as striking since, so it's worth going backward for a second look before you fill out your bridal registry. Hold out for cutlery from England in the 1950s from post-war manufacturers like Pride. Their silver-plate knife handles were embedded in white striped celluloid. Also check out the glamorous Swedish cutlery used on Scandinavian airlines in the late '50s and early '60s. (It was made by Jet Line.) But stick with stainless; so far there has been no market for vintage plastic flatware.

SURFBOARDS

Cool colors. Cool memories. Handmade fiberglass long boards from the 1960s rarely surface, but if you run into a

Dewey Weber, Greg Knoll, or Gordon and Smith, then go for it. They could be modern art for the living room or the incentive you need to get back on board. Think California and Long Island.

Don't overlook ultra-visual skateboards and snowboards, since they're on a roll as well.

SUZY COOPER

This English potter made her mark in the 1930s. She wanted "to create something for people who don't have a lot of money but who like nice things." Now her "nice things" have become prohibitively chic.

First Queen Mary and then the Duchess of Windsor collected these cheerful hand painted breakfast sets that sold for roughly a pound in high street china shops. Nowadays, the Hong Kong and New York markets are wild about her, and so are all kinds of people everywhere who just like "nice things."

Her best pieces are based on Bauhaus Cubist decorative influences and often show up at estate auctions. Since Suzy Cooper originally sold to the mass market, her china still shows up in estate, yard, and tag sales.

Tip: If American prices seem high, try Canadian antique malls. The prices will still seem high, but the dollar will work in your favor, especially if you bargain in American dollars.

TYPEWRITERS

Now that they've virtually achieved extinction status, typewriters have emerged as decorative art/sculpture of the computer generation. In fact, it's hard to pick up a late nineties decorating magazine and not see a typewriter carefully positioned as a casual aside.

Serious collectors seek out pre-1915 models, but later models have a growing fan club. The chicest are vintage Olivettis from Italy like the Lexicon 80 designed in 1948 or the Lexicon 83DL designed in 1976. Olivetti was known for using the top designers like Mario Bellini.

Portable Remingtons, Underwoods, and even early IBMs—like the 82M memory typewriter—or Eliot Noyes's Selectric and Model B electric typewriters from the early '60s also come with their own cache. No matter which one moves you, there are so many available that you can insist on mint condition.

If cache isn't sufficient cause to buy then there is another side benefit to decorating with retro-snazzy Italian or American typewriters—you can use them. Envelopes anyone? (Plus, unlike computers, you can find typewriters in unexpected colors like red.) If you're already a fan of Italian typewriter design, consider broadening your sights to include Olivetti's Summa 40 adding machines and calculators.

What Makes a House a Home?

"Home is in the eyes of old friends you can catch up with in an instant."

—Kelly Gordon, curator at the Hirshorn Museum

her collections:

Model sailboats
Vintage table runners
Ribbons
Ink, pastel, and watercolor landscapes
Occupied Japan basketry
Rookwood
Black and white photos of the Middle East

VINTAGE BIKER JEWELRY

Look for flea markets with proximity to retiring Hell's Angels. Vintage motorcycles are nice too.

VINTAGE CLOTHES

Save a bundle. Recycle any era you feel like wearing.

Vintage clothing stores are everywhere. Vintage fashion turns up at flea markets, pier shows, and secondhand stores. There is even a New York cable television show that lets you order secondhand outfits over the phone. Some stores let you buy old clothes by the pound. Individual pier shows and even museum collections specialize in the clothes by famous designers from way back when.

For immediate gratification, try vintage clothing stores, especially stores that give you unlimited access to the '60s and '70s. You'll be in good company.

It's no secret that some of the most well-known designers in the United States, France, and Italy prowl Manhattan's East Village vintage clothing stores like Smylon Nylon in search of the next important look. But chances are you won't even have to leave your own hometown. These days, the polyester '70s rule the streetwise fashion scene. Look for Pucci prints, cigarette pants, square-toed shoes, short fitted leather trench coats with wide lapels and skinny sleeves, or anything that you might have worn to a disco way back when. Conversely, a collection of country-club staples like sleeveless shifts, Bermuda sweaters, bouclé or beaded cardigans, jet set pearls, colorful alpaca golf sweaters, Lacoste, Lilly Pulitzer, and madras anything is invariably in vogue. And never, ever overlook military classics like authentic Navy pea coats, 1940s military storm coats, khakis, or Swedish Army anything.

Tip: Always shop for clothes very carefully. No matter how reasonable the price, check for stains like a hawk. If the store can't get a stain out, neither can you. Don't forget to smell everything before you buy it. You're not just checking for residual body odor but cigarettes. (Unless you live near one of the rare dry cleaners with an ozone machine, it's almost impossible to get the smell of cigarettes out of fiber if the garment was previously owned by a chain smoker.)

VISIBLE MAN, WOMAN, & COW

While they were never as popular with the masses as Barbie or GI Joe, or maybe because they weren't, Visible Man *and* Visible Woman now have a cult following all their own. In fact, those easy reference medical kits for junior internists are fast becoming heir transparent to the cool doll throne. However, you may want to hold out for a Visible Cow—complete with four stomachs to gaze upon instead of one.

VOODOO & SANTERIA COLLECTIBLES

The shapes and wrappings tell the spirit what to do, like beaded jazz riffs on just about any metaphysical topic.

Look for beaded, sequined flags and libation bottles, Mbondo baskets, wood, clay, and pigment cloth statues, wood and leather checkered Petwo drums, wizard spell books, or offering sail boats. The possibilities are endless. These folk objects often express amazing aesthetic and intellectual creativity and agility—encompassing Catholic saints, Masonic imagery, popular and political subcultures—all without missing a bead.

WELLER POTTERY

In its day, Weller was described as "utilitarian art pottery." However, the emphasis these days is currently on the art part. The Weller factory in Zanesville, Ohio, employed legendary designers like Charles Babcock Upjohn, Jacques Sicard, Frederick Rhead, and Gazo Fudji. These artists created vases, lamp bases, window boxes, planters, pitchers, ginger jars, bowls, and more. For the most dramatic collection, choose a single color, pattern, or designer.

WHITGO

Late 1950s cedar burned furniture with synthetic animal fur trim.

Hard to find, but hard to miss when you find it. This was the brand of furniture Elvis chose for Graceland. And you should shake, rattle, and roll it into your home if you can find what's left of it and it tickles your fancy.

WICKER FURNITURE

Straight off porches and summer cottages, American wicker was popular in the 1920s, 1930s, and again in the 1950s. Even a single piece can work casual wonders for all kinds of contemporary looks. As long as the weaving is in good condition all you need to do is repaint it annually. You may also want to add cushions made from vintage fabric.

WIRED STUFF

Bird cages, baskets, magazine racks, letter holders shaped like animals, and the like. Look for interesting shapes or think big. Like big wire mid-century side chairs.

WOODEN WONDERS

Maple. Walnut. Mahogany. Vintage wooden salad bowls have a special warmth and patina that improves with every year. Even when they crack, wooden bowls look good. But don't just think salad bowls, look for wooden bread baskets, antique wooden cheese boxes, wooden spoons, or pre-war Japanese wooden baskets carved from a single piece of teak or mahogany.

Chances are a vintage wooden piece with an irregular shape is handmade. If you should find an early small domestic wooden object like an egg cup, small container, or napkin ring that was turned on a lathe, it is usually called Treen. Pieces of this early wood are valuable, especially if they are in great condition or are carved from exceptional species of wood.

YIPPEE KAYAY

Stuff with a Western theme emerges from almost every decade. From the cowboy and Indian twin bed sheets of our childhoods to West High bandannas. Early steak house salt and pepper shakers, old saddles, scarf slides, watch fobs, and even cookie jars shaped like boots are all desirable.

PUTTING THINGS together

CHAPTER 6

Q. *What's in a Perfect Living Room?*

A. "I'd want it to have a fieldstone wall with a self-standing hooded '50s fireplace. A rough sixteenth-century French slab table. A pair of '50s blond wood Eames recliners. Abstract Expressionist paintings, tribal artifacts, and of course early American glass."

—Jim Oliveira, artist

The imprint of the alter-economy's distinctive style has been gaining momentum and influence despite the fact that these eclectic goods are outside of the commercial mainstream. Flea markets, pier shows, and even yard sales have become vital and acceptable alternatives for anyone decorating a home.

The alter-economy is helping to liberate us from programmed consumerism. While the world may be shrinking, our choices no longer have to be shrink-wrapped. As the tumbledown, mixed-up ending of the twentieth century looms, our choices are almost limitless.

With the visual vocabulary of the last hundred years spilled out in a chaotic display on wooden tables across the country, whatever you choose to pick up and rearrange can be seen in a new and possibly even a more reverent light.

So with all this candy to choose from, old-fashioned homogeneous collections now amount to nothing more than a snore. Truly obsessive collecting isn't pretty. In fact, it has more in common with a theme restaurant than it does with style.

Collecting every ceramic frog that ever croaked or every black velvet painting of Elvis ever created isn't as welcoming to friends visiting your home as you might imagine. Ditto hoarding five thousand refrigerator magnets or personally rounding up ten thousand swizzle sticks.

Overwhelming singular collections feel uncomfortable, especially when you could be putting together rooms that are far more personal and utilitarian.

This is why hunting and gathering in the new millennium is about anti-collection collectors traveling the depth and breadth of the twentieth century to create homes that enable them to rest and plug in their computers in peace and minimalism.

Given this contemporary urge to simplify and not quantify their lives, instead of 101 beer mugs of varying quality, modern collectors are assembling heterogeneous eclectic collections. Thus a single "collection" might include monogrammed wedding linens from the early 1900s, a single early, hand-carved wood pinecone, a vintage map of Africa, and several Murano glass vases from the 1960s to catch the light. Disparate, yet it can all work together to create a restful environment.

Flea style isn't about amassing acres of peeling painted furniture, deliberately cultivating clutter, or shabby chic. It's about creating evocative environments that could only belong to you. And no matter how corny this sounds, it's easy to do if you listen to your heart.

The shape and color of a French painted wood and metal coat-stand from the 1950s might help you get in touch with your inner decorating voice. Or the mood of an old Carole Lombard movie. But you've found your talisman—if you can ignore what is fashionable and wait until you spot an idiosyncratic intersection of shape, texture, color, and mood that moves your heart.

This won't be easy to find. Ask anyone over the age of thirty-five and you'll discover that decorating their home has been an ongoing odyssey to find the particular grouping of "toys" that works for them. In one decade of your life you can go through any number of decorating transformations from transient student to cozy Wild West to techno-minimal.

What you'll learn from this nonstop weeding and winnowing is the importance of asking yourself what made the grade as a keeper and why. In the end what makes a home uniquely yours are those pieces you could never bear to discard.

Q. *What's in a Perfect Loft?*

A. "A vintage leather club chair, definitely. A Chinese hanging painted glass scene lantern, a Chinese opium bed from the 1930s, outrageous Thai silk iridescent throw pillows, a low, tailored Eames couch, wide, low armless 1950s side chairs. For art, I'd hang Chinese advertising art posters from the 1930s, with a Chinese Art Deco rug in deep cobalt blue, and Noguchi lamps from the 1960s."

—Paul Krgowski, new media designer

Maybe its a wonderful old mirror you found on a vacation or a table that's been in your family since your father took his first step, or maybe its a vintage prayer rug you bought during the year you spent in an ashram. Wonderful pieces with a personal history and how you integrate them into your life are what combine to create a comforting environment.

Whether you're shaping a living room, guest room, or nursery, the underlying message of the alter-economy is always the same. The most successful rooms are those that are layered over time. No matter how many styles you blaze through in the middle, flea style is always malleable and never rejects what it can incorporate. If a chair is the wrong color, drape it with an oversized mover's blanket. If you're tired of your old china, see if mixing it up with different vintage patterns can give it new luster. If a family heirloom silver bowl looks too formal, fill it with lemons.

Don't be afraid of mixing eras, countries, or textures. Use your Heywood-Wakefield hutch from the 1950s to host a recent collection of Native American baskets. Collect Roseville pottery in a single color family but a variety of patterns. Add the luster of a sequined voodoo flag you brought back from Haiti to a blond 1950s Scandinavian living room instead of traditional glassware. Or bring home something that has no particular connection to anything else you own just because you had to have it. Even a large single object as arbitrary as an oversized worn vintage metal watering can, when left in the corner of your contemporary living room, can function as a sculptural sort of art—if it speaks to you.

You don't even need to go hog wild. Spare vintage luxury can be far more powerful than dense shelves of unedited stuff. One thing that lifts or comforts you for inexplicable reasons is all you need.

It's the Mix that Melds

It doesn't matter what period or country began an object's journey. Rearrange your collectibles to form a single great tableau. It doesn't have to be dramatic. The only caveat is that each piece in a collection be uniquely idiosyncratic, or of the best quality. Knickknacks rarely create a compelling ambiance on their own.

Experts recommend serious collectors keep their walls, floors, and furnishings neutral. That way you can develop your collections over time without risk of decorating warfare. The relaxed neutral palette the experts advocate is usually composed of clean-lined, canvas-covered furniture, sisal rugs, and white walls. For a luminous glow, serious nineteenth century antique collectors are often encouraged to turn to peach and honey walls instead of white. And some decorators even recommend strong colored walls like coral or bright yellow for collectors with a yen for dark furniture.

If you're going to integrate new possessions into your life, then you need to focus. For example, 1950s atomic print patterned sofas and turquoise walls don't so much spotlight a stuffed moose collection as shoot it down. So if you want to incorporate Depression glass, a wooden tennis racket, and a disco ball, go easy on the flocked velvet wallpaper. Your objective—if you choose to accept it—is to keep other distractions to a bare, tranquil minimum so the lines and colors of your talismen can shine through.

You can also incorporate any number of pieces by making good use of the cluster technique. This is the technique the majority of modern collectors swear by, and decorating magazines feature it month after month. Whiteware with whiteware. Wood with wood. Vintage flower prints mixed with striped and abstract print fabrics.

Hassocks and coffee tables make ideal surfaces to cluster objects on a favorite tray. Collect as many as twenty different silver candlestick holders to consolidate on an oversized silver tray for a lush, elegant look. Or fill a low woven tray with objects from the South Seas or the seashore.

Make any wall a decorative surface. Fill an entire living room wall with a mixture of fishing rods, sports plaques, snowshoes, and tennis rackets each placed for balance and shape. Or cover a wall with several versions of the same object like vintage ornamental bird cages or mirrors of every size and shape.

Use the wall of a stairwell as a surreal art gallery for wonderful but empty frames. Lean a series of surfboards against a wall. Organize a group of game boards with fascinating typefaces. Cluster miscellaneous musical instruments. Or frame black and white medical illustrations and hang them in a row.

If you're lucky enough to have a recessed spice enclave in your kitchen, don't bother with spices. Fill it with small art—like vintage salt and pepper shakers, toothpick holders, even a netsuke collection.

Q. *What's in a Perfect Kitchen?*

A. "That's easy. An old vintage Viking restaurant stove, an oiled cherry wood island with a stainless steel top and a slate floor. Plus I'd want an original post-war Waring stainless steel blender, Yellow ware mixing bowls, and 1920s Czechoslovakian kitchen furniture."

—John Nathanson, architect

Or Break It Up

The days of formal matched bedroom or even dining room sets are over. Today, not only are you allowed to break up matched sets, it can look oddly stuffy if you don't.

Form and function are now up to you—and only you. China cabinets, once a staple of the dining room, are showing up in foyers—and in bedrooms. Bedroom armoires are now doubling as entertainment centers in living rooms.

Old wicker porch chairs have moved into spacious bathrooms. Office reception and conference desks and chairs from the '40s and '50s are finding their way into not just home offices but living and dining rooms as well.

Texture Is Tactile

Mixing textures is another way to integrate all kinds of things into your home.

Take textiles. To make a bed feel warm layer a wool patterned blanket over a trapunto quilt at the foot of bed over an Egyptian cotton duvet. Toss a '50s print throw pillow against vintage monogrammed pillowcases.

Fill a crystal claw-footed bowl with vintage marbles. Cover a wooden bureau top with a mix of exotic textures, like an old metal money box, long strands of African glass trading beads, and a small vase of lush blooming peonies.

Think Alternative Use

Don't be bound by what other people used things for long ago—or even recently. Old cast-iron Christmas tree stands make impressive candlestick holders for huge pillar candles. Oversized sports trophies work as well with flowers as they do empty.

Recycle wonderful old fabrics originally used for drapes into placemats, wrapping for presents, upholstery, pillows, or turn them into a vest.

The possibilities for revisiting are infinite. Envision a red Olivetti typewriter as modern sculpture on a sideboard. Organize an expanding sunglasses collection with a quirky '50s tie rack. Let a wooden or even a taxidermied snarling lion's head hold your keys. Use a handmade ladder to display a collection of immaculate monogrammed vintage linens in a guest bathroom. Or envision a '50s tulle prom dress as a romantic lampshade.

Try this three-pronged mantra to imagine using something you're drawn to for something other than what it is.

1. **What could it hold?**

2. **Where could it hang?**

3. **What else could it be?**

Authenticity as Art

Horn vessels. Antlers. Vintage porcelain bathtub feet. Cast-iron grills from heating fixtures peeling with layers of old paint. Matte silver, black iron, hammered steel hardware. Scientific instruments. Vintage aluminum mailboxes.

Nowadays, all kinds of weathered hardware and bits of natural history are considered objects worth coveting.

Hold out for bits of old cast iron that move you. Curious shells. Or lengths of rusted barbed wire you can nail to your wall in your favorite I Ching configurations.

Think Wunderkammer

Create a home museum. In the late sixteenth and early seventeenth centuries, it was popular to have a cabinet or table in your house dedicated to as many one-of-a-kind natural wonders of personal significance as the family could muster. These were called *wunderkammer*, and eventually these private collections became the predecessors of public museums.

House objects that have deep history for you in a curio cabinet. Look for a metal display case. Or heap a lacquer tray near your bed with flotsam, jetsam, and sponges from the distant seas, dried Spanish moss from a road trip to Savannah, or a particularly lucky wishbone.

Showcase a little archeology beside your bed. Collect wonderful natural objects from the strange depths of primordial history, as well as objects of innate wonder. Shells that look like your grandfather. Bones rumored to come from sea monsters. Or any objects that cause wonder.

Q. *What's in a Perfect Space?*

A. "The perfect space for me would be two rooms with perfect proportions and rough plaster walls. Everything scrubbed. Concrete floors. Comfortable leather furniture. Shelf units, because books are very, very important. I could use the shelves for stone paperweights, stone obelisks, stone lions, and anything else that has withstood time by weathering well. For a rug I'd want a very flat geometric 1930s rug in a rich color. But for lighting I'd want some perky Lucite rod 1950s pole lights with dimmers. Lighting is critical, but no track lights. Ever."

—Frank Rosa, owner of 20th Century Designs

Spiritual Spaces Make a House a Home

Nowadays, more people go to church on Super Bowl Sunday than watch the big game. If you share this return to faith, you might want to consider adding a spiritual component to your current decor no matter how spartan or technology-driven your master plan may be. Religious artifacts can be vital to creating balance in the midst of a bank of television screens, monitors, and fax machines.

You choose the message. Laughing Buddhas mix well. So do strings of oversized wooden rosary beads or Mosque mosaics. Contrast is compelling. Finding a place to hang, store, or enshrine a single relic can help anchor the future.

Appropriate Eccentricity

Need something amazing with a history and an immediacy that will help you reconstruct your own personal mosaic in a flash? Poke around a flea market or an antique mall or even a pawn shop. You'll know exactly what you're looking for when you see it—especially when you find the totem that speaks to you. From a vintage moose head, to a set of Italian glass homeopathic jars, to a life preserver bearing an evocative yacht's name. When it's meant to be yours alone, you'll know.

Stranger than that, when you find your mysterious talisman you'll know exactly where to place it.

Think Jung

One Jungian theory holds that whether we know it or not, each of us has a shrine in our home that speaks volumes about our inner values. Look for things that always move with you, no matter how often you move. The things that reflect your values always manage to get hung on the wall or laid out in the same way. They're a psychic snapshot and a clue to your inner mosaic.

Collections also reveal strangely intimate information about the shapes, forms, and textures that move you. Which raises the whole issue of content—which is quite another kettle of fish, entirely.

Be Who You Really Are

Collect what you like most from all those reruns. You can even watch several channels at once by mixing a high-tech living room with a low-tech kitchen.

You can be a '90s minimalist in the bedroom and a '50s homemaker deluxe in the kitchen. Stock it with Donna Reed aprons, Pyrex mixing bowls, brushed aluminum canisters, and Bakelite-handled silverware. Power up the low-tech way with an electric percolator, a toaster, souvenir salt and pepper shakers, a warm-and-fuzzy cookie jar, turquoise and watermelon tablecloths, and a rotary phone on the counter.

Or keep your kitchen a tribute to the microwave decade and turn your living room into an homage to '60s passion pit sophisticates with a little chrome and a lot of glass. Toss cosmic-colored Marimekko pillows against your white duck sofa, or better yet blow up color-dotted plastic throw pillows. Lay down a shaggy white Flokati or color-drenched Rya rugs. Leave Lucite laying around. Collect fondue forks.

Mantelpiece Mantras

If you've got a fireplace, use that mantel. It's a still life canvas par excellence. It's possibilities are infinite. Particularly when it comes to housing objects. Hang a big find like a candelabra sconce (or the fish that got away) over the mantel. Create a shrine to rock and roll, wanderlust, or a meaningful shape, texture, or era. Your entire collection of same-size crystal geodes, Rookwood, pickle castors, or barn pulleys would each be wonderfully showcased.

Use the ledge to hold a heterogeneous collection of eclectic, strange smallish objects that are meaningful to you, like a single ceramic tile from a Mosque, a silver flute, and a special postcard.

There's No Place Like Home

The mix creates the mood.

Homes like that of Los Angeles interior designer Cheryl Brantner are created by knowing what to pick from each decade—and where to put it. The mood she creates is a spare, spacious mix of decades, continents, and technology. It isn't simply about contrast, texture, and color, but about choosing carefully and artfully, too.

Brantner harmoniously stacks fresh cut logs in her living room near her grand piano, cattycorner from a distressed leather club chair found on the streets of Paris. A vintage French metal table from the '40s is heaped with her favorite art books. On the other side of the room, Murano glass from the '60s mingles with the evocative warmth of a fluted burled English Deco armoire.

Brantner's extensive collection of natural artifacts, as well as her twentieth-century collection of Weller and Catalina white ware, carved horn, ivory, art books, Spratling, and Georg Jensen objects reappear in all the rooms of her home, creating a flow of mood.

American
Markets
& Meccas

CHAPTER 7

In flea markets,

as in peep shows, there are always surprises.

—Richard Merkin

You can't see anything when you're asleep.

—Toots Shor, legendary nightclub owner, rumored to have slept very little

Flea Meccas

You'll find that even with an ever-diversifying population, our regional legacy still contributes to our collective conscience.

Yankee thrift. Midwest pragmatism. West Coast funk. Southern gothic eccentricity. Think-big Texas scale. Northwest organic. In fact, it seems inherently American to want to pull from all of these legacies to celebrate experimentation, invention, and self-determination. These days, we want to have a little of everything.

Which is why the alter-economy scene is constantly in flux as dealers and pickers drive from one end of the country to the other in search of just about anything.

In addition to flea markets, antique boutiques, secondhand stores, and antique malls, there are now whole towns that resemble flea markets. The list below is a combination of some of the seasonal shows, local shows, extravaganza and pier shows, unusual places, auctions, thrift shops, and towns that are worth investigating. The only criteria that unites this listing is the presence of consistently eccentric goods that represent both the twentieth century and the region. Use it as a representative list of what's happening in the world of hunting and gathering near you. But never go to any of them with a shopping list set in stone. It can prevent you from seeing what's there that might be even more amazing.

You might also want to begin keeping a notebook of flea markets, junk stores, thrift shops, or regional events that sound intriguing. Think of it as an adventure journal.

ALABAMA

Scottsboro

UNCLAIMED BAGGAGE CENTER
509 West Willow
☎ (205) 259-5753
Mon.–Thurs. 8 A.M.–5 P.M., Friday 8 A.M.–7 P.M.

The Unclaimed Baggage Center is a curious facet of new millennium shopping. It's at least worth thinking about in a philo-
sophical sense even if you don't go for a drive-by. This store
(and a smaller one across the street) is where the unclaimed
contents of lost freight as well as the luggage from airlines
eventually ends up.

This store sells everything from the computers and monitors
ordered but never picked up to top-of-the-line golf clubs, at
one-third to one-half the original prices. And clothes—well,
you can only imagine.

The possibilities are myriad because people do tend to travel
with their best clothes, cameras, and perfumes. However
don't forget these bags were unclaimed, which can also mean
the lost luggage wasn't as valuable to the previous owners as
the opportunity to collect the insurance for their lost baggage.

ARIZONA

Retirees started moving to this sunny state in droves after the
invention of air conditioning in the 1940s. Nowadays a surreal

number of RVs flaunt the bumper sticker "We're Spending Our Children's Inheritance." Much like Florida, upper middle class retirees account for a remarkable number of antiques finds, from silver to furniture that they get rid of once they moved to Arizona.

Bisbee

Historic old Bisbee is twenty miles from Tombstone, five miles from Mesa, and ninety miles south of Tucson. Yet the Bisbee Chamber of Commerce regularly compares its Victorian hillside houses and charms to those of Italy and Switzerland!

This is a genuine old copper mining town with great bird watching, a botanical cactus garden, used book stores, craft shops, a fiber guild coop, numerous art galleries, and the Shady Dell RV Park. This is a fully restored vintage trailer park with '40s and '50s Airstream, El Ray, Spartan, and Crown aluminum traveling trailers. Bisbee is also the kind of small, friendly town where mail can only be delivered to box numbers. So most mornings you'll find local residents and shop owners gathering at the main post office with a coffee mug in hand.

Funky and upscale antique stores sell furniture from a variety of decades, silver, and antiques, as well as cowboy collectibles, jukeboxes, and strange lamps. On the weekends up to seven vendors sell household stuff in Peddlers Alley. (It's a small alley—so don't count on more vendors showing up in good weather.)

BISBEE ANTIQUES & COLLECTIBLES   *Antique Boutique*
3 Main Street
☎ (520) 432-4320
Call for hours, they vary

The owner says movie stars like it here—and well they should. It's a nifty source for high-end, first choice collectibles like Lustreware, silver-edged Roseville, and entire sets of unusual sterling flatware. And better yet, all their antiques and collectibles are *guaranteed* to be authentic!

FLYING SAUCER   *Antique Boutique*
26 Brewary Avenue
☎ (520) 432-3567
Open by appointment or by chance

From kitsch to restored pinball machines from the '30s through the '50s, this singularly eccentric store is usually one step ahead of the curve—in more ways than one. The owner's main area of interest is the 1940s, but all things eccentric have a way of turning up here. Especially psycho-ceramics.

FUNKY JUNQUE   *Antique Boutique*
120 Naco Road
☎ (520) 432-2975
Mon.–Fri. 10 A.M.–5 P.M., weekends 9 A.M.–6 P.M.

Sort of a general store for the millennium. Expect used metaphysical books. Vintage cowboy duds. Ghostbusters pup tents. Beatles and Star Wars curtains. Yul Brynner plates. However, the rest of this generalist style store is stocked with the kind of used utilitarian goods that local residents might need, like pots and pans.

CALIFORNIA

Californians practically invented eclectic abandon as a decorating motif. They are enthusiastic about the Arts and Crafts movement, yet almost intuitive in their understanding of the '50s and '60s.

San Francisco specializes in eclecticism with a vintage Asian accent. Meanwhile Southern California has its own interpretation of how to mix up the entire century in unexpected tableaus. Numerous high-end vintage shops throughout Los Angeles, but particularly along La Brea, La Cienega, and Montana Avenue cater to a fascination with scavenging the millennium by providing the best of the twentieth century from around the world. In other words, everybody wants everything. Which may be why tag sales, yard sales, and flea markets are so popular in Los Angeles.

Even traditional shopping in Los Angeles offers surprises worth seeing just for their educational value. For example, shops like Blackman and Crews specialize in international twentieth-century antiques juxtaposed with austere French metal furniture, while stores like Retro on La Brea sell a comprehensive collection of remarkable '60s glass vases in every nuance of the rainbow.

Los Angeles

LIZ'S ANTIQUE STORE
453 South La Brea Boulevard
☎ (213) 939-4403
Mon.–Sat.

Vintage Hardware

It could simply be an old light plate from one vantage point. Then again, if you had five of them resting against a ledge, well-worn vintage light plates are suddenly transformed into art. This highly concentrated store of nothing but fixtures and hardware is a wealth of ideas and inspiration. You'll see the beauty of utilitarian forms when they're thoughtfully separated from function.

Liz's Antique Store stocks every old peeled paint heating vent imaginable. Buckets of bathtub claw feet that might date back to the ice age are newfound art. (Ditto for drawer pulls, tiebacks, vintage aluminum mail boxes, etc.)

They sell a catalog featuring reproductions, but you should go there in person. Once you've seen it all, you'll have new ideas for what to look for at yard sales and flea markets.

THE LOS ANGELES MODERNISM SHOW
Santa Monica Civic Auditorium
Main Street at Pico Boulevard
☎ (310) 455-2886
Early May; call for details

You have to see it to believe it. The L.A. Modernism Show is a visual textbook of almost every style and decade imaginable.

This is a high-end market that covers almost every decorative art and furniture movement in the twentieth century. Bauhaus, Art Nouveau, Cubism, Pop Art, Futurism, Deco Moderne, Machine Age, WPA, Fifties Arts and Crafts, and architectural design.

This kind of all-encompassing show is an excellent chance to get a good look at mint condition modern antiques, see what trends are emerging, or simply learn more about any category that interests you. Prepare to have your senses overloaded by astounding stashes of the best of the best. A recent show included astounding collections of American ceramic producers like Rookwood, Grueby, and Newcomb, great examples of Modernism (every cocktail shaker imaginable) and what looked like $12 million worth of Tiffany lamps. Chances are you won't get a bargain, but at least you'll have fun.

Burbank

THE BURBANK MONTHLY ANTIQUE MARKET
1001 Riverside Drive (at Main Street, across from the L.A.
  Equestrian Center)
☎ (310) 455-2886
Fourth Sunday of every month, 8 A.M.–3 P.M.

This is a great market if you don't mind paying top dollar for first-rate small things like Catalina or Bauer pottery, watches, fabric, fountain pens, vintage photographs, entertainment memorabilia, and Indian silver. And despite its small size, this indoor (air-conditioned) market attracts a serious crowd. The serious and highly professional dealers have quite a devoted following.

Hancock Park

CHASEE DE LA BREA

Corner of 6th Street and South La Brea Boulevard

☎ (714) 631-3232

First Friday of every month, 5 P.M.–11 P.M.

While night markets are popular in Asia, this is L.A.'s first and only one. It's a parking lot by day but it's in a convenient Hancock Park location, which makes it ideal for nocturnal pursuits. Plus, night shoppers will find Chasee de La Brea densely packed with classic California pottery, Bakelite jewelry, vintage luggage, and velvet paintings. Don't expect much in the way of big stuff like furniture. On the other hand, valet parking is available and so is delivery. Plus, it's catered by a well-known local restaurant on La Brea Boulevard.

Given Chasee de La Brea's evening hours and its opportune location, you may want to walk to one of the many trendy restaurants that line South La Brea Boulevard. Remember to make reservations beforehand; this *is* L.A.

Long Beach

THE LONG BEACH ANTIQUE & COLLECTIBLE MARKET

Veteran's Memorial Stadium

(Conant Street between Lakewood and Clark)

☎ (213) 655-5703

Third Sunday of the month, 6:30 A.M.–3 P.M. (free before 8 A.M.)

This is a big meat-and-potatoes generic market that has it all: from antique prayer rugs and wonderful engravings of the human skull to great California pottery and one-of-a-kind stuff. You can also count on lots of lighting fixtures, Hollywood memorabilia, used clothing, quilts, autograph books, door-knobs, hardware, and sports memorabilia galore.

A word to the wise: get there very early if you're looking for indoor or outdoor furniture. (Furniture is sold on the market's far left side as you face away from the stadium.)

Pasadena

THE ROSE BOWL
1001 Rose Bowl Drive
☎ (213) 588-4411
Second Sunday of every month, 6 A.M.–4:30 P.M.

The Rose Bowl is a competitive, crowded scene with such a rabid following that you may feel like an alien if you're not striding purposefully toward the back lot with a pull cart behind you. If, like many movie stars, you're making the pilgrimage to the Rose Bowl primarily to find vintage top-stitched blue jeans, head toward the right as the market forks near the entrance. There are over 1,600 dealers, so make plans where to meet if you and a friend get separated.

Furniture, strange lamps, and any hope of a nearby parking space go quickly. Plus, if you're not careful, you'll miss the fork in the market that separates the antiques and collectibles from the junk. But wherever you look you'll see aisle after aisle of classic American art pottery like White, Yellow, Fiesta, and Bauer ware. Used and vintage clothing are also a popular staple and can range from authentic silver firefighter's jackets to polyester classics from the '70s. Garage and attic style goods from lazy Susans to ashtrays and aprons predominate. And there are definitely bargains to be had in almost every category.

Shoppers at this market are so fanatical that it pays to have your strategy down to a science before you get out of your car. Be polite. Know what you're after. And scan each row carefully so you don't miss what other people are buying. This is a market where you can spot trends in the making by keeping your eye on what other shoppers are carrying home in those pull carts.

And yes, the Rose Bowl really is set in a "bowl" of dazzling California terrain known as an arroyo. Look up occasionally. The view is panoramic.

Santa Monica

SANTA MONICA OUTDOOR ANTIQUE & COLLECTIBLE MARKET
Airport Avenue (the Santa Monica Airport)
☎ (213) 933-2511
Fourth Sunday of every month
You don't even have to bother looking for a parking space—you can literally fly into this high-end but casual Santa Monica flea market. It's very small, but you'll find a far hipper collection of stuff here than you would at an average market. (Dealers cater

to the surrounding Westside communities of well-to-do producers, directors, screenwriters, and other local residents.)

Expect unusual housewares and decorative accessories from the '40s, '50s, and '60s, great California pottery, jazzy modernist vintage fabrics, and a fun crowd. Just don't expect amazing deals. Expect consistently interesting and eccentric stuff at darn close to blue-book prices. Get there as early as possible; after 8 A.M. it's picked over by other dealers.

San Francisco

NAOMI *Antique Boutique*
1817 Polk Street
☎ (415) 775-1207

Naomi is a Mecca for anyone with an interest in vintage dinner and artware pottery. This store specializes in American dinnerware from 1930–1960. And American art pottery from 1890–1960. It's packed to the gills with some of the best mint-condition pieces imaginable—including rare colors and unusual serving pieces.

DE VERA *Antique Boutique*
334 Gough Street, and 384 Hayes Street
☎ (415) 558-8865

These two spare, striking boutiques are a block apart and each offers a spare collection of strange, fascinating highly eclectic vintage objects. De Vera is well worth visiting just to see what combinations the eye will be drawn to next. One shop sells art glass and the other sells esoteric objects. The owner has an exceptional aesthetic standard.

Santa Barbara

LOST HORIZON BOOKSTORE *Bookstore*
703 Anacapa Street
☎ (805) 962-4606
Mon.–Sat. 10 A.M.–6 P.M., Sun. 11 A.M.–5 P.M.

Discovering a cache of great collectible books is always a treat whether they are new or old. If your area doesn't have a used bookstore and you're looking for a book about almost any kind of collectible (obscure or otherwise) then this is a great store to visit or call. They're known for their extensive collection of reference books about everything imaginable—including many volumes that are used or out of print. Just a fraction of the topics covered include Art Deco tableware, Bentwood and metal furniture, early Utah furniture, buffalo pottery, and women silversmiths.

Towns That Would Be Flea Markets

A flea market is an odd sprawling tent city that takes shape overnight. As more and more dealers arrive and set up tables, aisles begin to take shape, then whole blocks.

That same Brigadoon-like transformation is happening to more and more towns across the country as antique stores, secondhand shops, junk stores, antique malls, and seasonal events take over whole towns—or at least whopping big chunks of them. These days, as the economy takes curious turns, towns are reinventing themselves as nouvelle flea markets.

Some like Mt. Dora in Florida are the result of an economy that has emerged in response to the crowds that visit the seasonal flea market. Others like Hudson, New York, and Walnut, Iowa, are a result of the sheer volume of goods from surrounding communities and estate sales, while others like Mesa, Arizona, may be a result of tourists in search of authenticity they can bring home.

CONNECTICUT

Farmington

FARMINGTON ANTIQUES WEEKEND
Polo Grounds
From I-84 take exit 39, nine miles west of Hartford
☎ (203) 677-7862
Second weekend of June and Labor Day weekend

Farmington is the more organized and suburban version of Brimfield. Comparisons aside, if you're decorating an old house or looking for one-of-a-kind Americana, then the Farmington market is quite a must-do scene. This well-organized event attracts many designers, decorators, and store owners. Held on a polo field twice a year, Farmington is quite the event. However, it is still Connecticut, so look for furniture like Bentwood chairs, wicker, painted high-back Hitchcock chairs, tin toys, old telephones, and household goods. In short, all sorts of traditional American country classics and antiques can be found. Particularly garden furniture.

Woodbury

WOODBURY ANTIQUES & FLEA MARKET
Route 6
from I-84 take Exit 15
Weekends

This market is on the outskirts of a town known for antique and specialty shops—which may be why Woodbury attracts up to seventy dealers. Not much on atmosphere—at first squint it could pass for a trampled field. Woodbury Market has a devoted following for good reason: their very friendly, knowledgeable dealers. So once you wind your way past the new stuff, check out the tools, kitchen collectibles, duck decoys, books, and one-of-a-kind weird loot.

DISTRICT OF COLUMBIA

Georgetown

THE GEORGETOWN FLEA
Wisconsin and S Street
☎ (800) 625-7553
Sunday 9 A.M.–5 P.M.

This is a local weekend market very popular with diplomats' wives. Over one hundred dealers sell all sorts of furniture, vintage clothing, glass, books, art, and costume jewelry. Word is European women in particular go there for costume jewelry. In any case, this schoolyard venue is quite the local scene. The market closes in January and February.

FLORIDA

Unloading furniture and household goods brought with them from up north is invariably the first step in the life of recent Florida retirees. From furniture to clothes to china, it's out with the old and in with the new. Florida is the ultimate modern treasure chest, from mint condition beaded cashmere sweater sets to Russel Wright and 1950s furniture.

No matter where you go in Florida, you should always look through the Yellow Pages under "Thrift Stores" and "Antique Malls." Besides an amazing lineup of flea markets throughout the state, you'll find thrift shops in Pensacola, consignment stores in Palm Beach, or antique malls on Route 19 that will leave your adrenaline supercharged.

Mt. Dora

RENNINGER'S FLORIDA TWIN MARKET
20651 Highway 441
Just southeast of Mt. Dora in Lake County, twenty miles north of
　Orlando in central Florida
☎ (904) 383-3141
Weekends, in season

Renninger's is spread out over 115 acres and is divided into two sections. An antique market at the bottom of a hill sells one-of-a-kind art objects, American and imported period furniture, and vintage gadgets. At the top of the hill there's a flea market for conversation pieces and bargains.

Amazing twentieth-century collectibles end up here thanks to retiring couples from every state in the union. Mt. Dora is invariably cited as the largest source of excellent "antiques and collectibles" in the country. (Including the best of the collections from retirees who furnished their homes in the early '50s and raised their children in the '60s!) This is where the circuit begins for many, many, many dealers who start here and then work their way down the state and then back up— or who take the goods they purchase here across the country from Texas to Idaho to New Hampshire.

Check out the whole town of Mt. Dora while you're there. Although it's increasingly veering toward more low-end stores, you'll find block after block of restaurants, antique stores, bookstores, chic boutiques, and miles of lakeside parks. To complete your tour of the last century, stay at the 112-year-old Lakeside Inn!

Antique and collectible shows are held the third weekend of every month, 9 A.M.–5 P.M. Mixed markets including new stuff are held every weekend. Renninger's Extravaganzas are held in January and February.

Webster

WEBSTER FARMER'S FLEA MARKET
Highway 47 North (at the county fairgrounds)
☎ (904) 793-3551
Monday 6:30 A.M.–2:30 P.M.

Their slogan is "If you want it—it's here" and they're not kidding.

You just have to do a little walking—give or take forty acres or so. You'll have to wade through vistas of fruit and vegetables, wholesale hats, hand-decorated sweatshirts, alligator-tipped pencils, and nurses anxious to pierce your ears for a small fee, but eventually you'll get to the antiques and twentieth-century collectibles. When you do find them, it's worth it—especially in the summer, when the prices are amazing. Look for eccentric one-of-a-kind stuffed fish trophies, vintage golf clubs, Formica tables, furniture, linens, patio furniture, African masks and 1940s and 1950s treasures galore.

When you call their phone number, the menu lets you select handy direction information.

Fort Myers

FLEA MASTERS FLEA MARKET
4135 Anderson Avenue
From State 82, take exit 23, one mile west from I-75
☎ (941) 334-7001
Fri.–Sun.

Flea Masters is a basic rambling, indoor/outdoor Florida trash and treasure grove with at least eight hundred dealers to check out. Almost every category of twentieth-century antiques and collectibles show up here, from housewares to furniture (as well as a lot of new—sometimes strange—

merchandise and many handmade crafts.) It's not a major market on the order of Mt. Dora, and the tube-sock quotient is high. However, you'll also invariably leave with something truly unexpected at a great price. Especially if you go in the summer, when prices are rock bottom.

Orlando

FLEA WORLD
Highway 17–92
Between Orlando and Sanford
☎ (407) 647-3976
Fri.–Sun.

Not only is this 104-acre venue conveniently located near Disney World, occasionally it's nearly as crowded—only with adults. Probably because few flea markets offer this many other distractions, including bingo, a hairdresser, and a farmers market. Go for an hour and you could end up spending the day. There are at least 1,200 booths, and best of all, air conditioning.

Amidst all the new and discounted merchandise and diversions, you'll find booths featuring nineteenth-century antiques and twentieth-century collectibles from tools and fire fighting paraphernalia to golf memorabilia and garage-sale leftovers galore—at terrific prices. Like many Florida markets, however, you'll find far more collectible booths once the summer months are over and tourist season is back in force.

St. Petersburg

THE MUSTANG DRIVE-IN FLEA MARKET
Park Blvd. between 73rd and 74th Streets
Wed.–Sun. 6 A.M.–2 P.M.

This is the real deal—so get there at dawn (especially on Sunday) and don't forget your flashlight. "Dealers" deal from the top, the trunks, and the sides of their cars, pick-ups, or RVs. Expect exceptional, only-in-Florida prices on all kinds of curious housewares, furniture, toys, and even international artifacts from this ever-changing collection of non-professionals, pickers, and quasi-professionals. At the far edge of the market, you'll also find an international farmer's bazaar of seasonal produce featuring mangoes, plantains, Asian herbs, and bolts of unusual Asian textiles.

Dealers from many of the St. Petersburg antique malls arrive at Mustang very early, so set your alarm clock and don't dawdle at any one blanket once you're there.

PATTY AND FRIENDS *Antique Mall*
1225 9th Street North
☎ (813) 821-2106
Daily

Three townhouses make up this must-visit antique mall. You'll find practically every category of mint condition Depression and carnival glass, Roseville jardinieres, Moorish madness, Yellow ware, stoneware, Fire King, Fiesta ware, primitive pieces, train accessories, and more. They also feature one of the best selections in the country of reconditioned electric fans from the '40s!

Unless you're especially interested in country pieces or nineteenth century collectibles, you may want to start at the two-story townhouse, where you'll find Patty herself. Then cut across the yard and around the side of a building to find Person's Antiques Too. The owner has a great eye for unusual pieces from crystal balls and Chinoiserie to lava heads and Candlewick glass breakfast sets.

Ft. Lauderdale

THUNDERBIRD SWAP MEET
3121 W. Sunrise Boulevard
☎ (305) 792-1329
Wed.–Sun.

The lure of this magnetic attraction is that this huge swap meet is also one heck of a yard sale. Unlike many flea markets these days, Thunderbird attracts non-professionals, who arrive with blankets and the truly unexpected, as well as seasoned professionals selling everything from vintage golf clubs to amazing Depression glass. Also no surprise since we're talking Florida, you'll also run into bingo, surreal amounts of new stuff, auctions, and live music.

Tampa

METROPOLIS TWENTIETH CENTURY
   ANTIQUES
Bay to Bay Boulevard
☎ (813) 839-1769
Tues.–Sun.

Antique Boutique

This is one of the best of Tampa's many vintage stores. This 1,800-square foot industrial-sized space is divided into rooms by era: including a '60s, a '50s, and a '30s Deco room. All this organization makes it easy to go straight to their '50s refurbished refrigerators, streamlined chrome toasters, ice crushers, rotary phones, table fans, and '50s future-style clocks that actually work. To replay the '60s ad infinitum, check out their collection of Saarinen tulip chairs, big light bulb lamps, and Lucite everything.

GEORGIA

Savannah

There are so many prestigious and unusual antique stores in Savannah that the Visitor's Bureau publishes a special brochure with descriptions and a map to help you find them all. This guide is available in almost every shop; or stop by the Visitor's Center. The map can help you find specific antique shops devoted to vintage erotica, maritime books, or birdhouses.

Be warned, locals take antiques and yard sales very seriously here (as do the local dealers, who often manage to get there first). Flow blue china, wicker furniture, and real antiques are the grail.

KELLER'S FLEA MARKET
Highway 17 South
from I-95 take Exit 16

☎ (912) 927-4808

Fri.–Sun. until 6 P.M. depending on the heat

If you're in dire need of a truly rusted piece of large farm machinery, a screeching parrot, a baby gerbil, or a slightly used computer keyboard, then this rustic flea and farmer's market is for you. Even if none of the above categories appeal to you in the slightest, you can still appreciate why local dealers make the occasional journey to see what's up at this sprawling scene. In the midst of country pandemonium you'll also find the occasional cut glass Marie Therese chandelier, primitive pine tables, as well as used baseball bats, cast-iron frying pans, and all sorts of miscellaneous domestic finds.

Keller's Market is worth a peek if you're in the neighborhood or traveling through it—but probably not worth a special trip from out of state. It's a rambling market consisting of a series of wooden structures. The structures where vintage goods are sold are located toward the back of the property furthest from the main road.

ATTIC ANTIQUES   *Antique Boutique*

224 West Bay Street

☎ (912) 236-4879

Located on the street level of a renovated old cotton warehouse facing the river near trendy River Street, this funky, well-edited vintage shop is a definite find. Jammed to the gills with everything from affordable "real" antiques, to well used golf clubs, tennis rackets, Visible Man, flow blue china, and a $1 toy bin, this laid back shop even has a provenance of its own.

It used to be the site of the practically legendary piano bar once owned by Joe Odun and Emma Kelly in "that book." Even the marks on the floor where Emma Kelly played her piano are still embedded in the back of this small shop.

FIESTA AND MORE

Antique Boutique

224 West Bay Street
☎ (912) 238-1060

Downstairs from Attic Antiques, this popular shop claims to have the largest collection of Fiesta ware in the country. In addition to Fiesta, they stock Depression glass, coins, Oriental rugs, and cut glass from the 1800s. Call to receive a catalog.

ATLANTA FLEA MARKET

5360 Peachtree Industrial Boulevard
☎ (770) 458-0456
Fri. and Sat. 11 A.M.–7 P.M., Sun. 12 P.M.–7 P.M.

Not the most consistent market, but with 150 booths all agree this is definitely one of the biggest markets in the South. It's a random mix of Americana, country classics, and "gift items." Since Arts and Crafts and industrial designers don't tend to be as highly valued in the South, you might be able to get a better price when the occasional twentieth-century classic turns up. Although these days less and less is undervalued—unless it's the last day.

ILLINOIS

St. Charles

KANE COUNTY ANTIQUES FLEA MARKET
Kane County Fairgrounds
Randall Road south of Rt. 64
☎ (708) 377-2252
First weekend of every month
Sat. 1 P.M.–5 P.M., Sun. 7 A.M.–4 P.M.

A Midwest classic known for attracting local decorators, serious collectors, and the Chicago crowd. It doesn't have quite the spread of vintage goods it was once known for, but it's still a friendly, rambling market with all kinds of furniture, kitchen appliances, china patterns, blankets, toys, vintage tools, '50s memorabilia, game boards, classic dinnerware, fine jewelry—and a lot of discount new merchandise. Over nine hundred dealers participate, so you can be sure something will catch your eye.

SANDWICH ANTIQUES MARKET
Fairgrounds, State Road 34
☎ (312) 227-4464
Sat.–Sun. 8 A.M.–4 P.M.

The prestigious Sandwich Antiques Market is a little over an hour from Chicago, through cornfields and a small heartland style township. The dealers come from all across the country, so don't expect "typical" Midwest finds—with the exception of old farm tools, which are well represented. Instead, anticipate cherry and mahogany furniture dating back to the early 1900s, brass doorknobs, Tiffany glass window frames, and lots of rugs requiring serious cleaning. Many shoppers go there exclusively for Depression glass and 1950s china patterns. The best finds could be the more curious nostalgia pieces from old stores like butcher block tables from local shops.

INDIANA

Centerville

WEBBS ANTIQUE MALL   *Antique Mall*
200 W. Union Street
Two miles south of 1-70, exit 145
☎ (317) 855-5542

This 70,000 square-foot Midwest antique mall is so big that regulars grumble it may have become too big. The quality is not quite what it used to be, but the sheer size of the place means you'll undoubtedly leave with something or other. It could be a quilt, it could be a piece of holiday decorating madness, or a mint condition Yellow ware bowl. But if you don't find a major score, then mosey on a little further. The whole town around the Centerville market is filled with even more antique malls and flea markets.

IOWA

Generations of Iowa families stored their old stuff in the attic and the basement. Now no dealer in his right mind ever fails to hit the brakes for a yard sale and especially for estate sales in Iowa.

Local enthusiasts and dealers hunt for quilts, Wattsware pottery in the Red Apple pattern, and farm collectibles. An immigrant trunk at an estate sale is considered quite a red-letter find.

WHAT CHEER, LARRY NICHOLSON'S COLLECTORS PARADISE FLEA MARKET

Keokuk County Fairgrounds I-80, Exit 201 South

☎ (515) 634-2109

First Sunday in May, August, and October

A few years ago What Cheer, as the market is called by regulars, was known as a wonderful market for the kind of old furniture and primitives you could take home and refinish, refurbish, or reupholster. It still is, but these days they also sell their fair share of reproductions. Despite the assault of "new stuff" and reproductions there is enough vintage furniture, and primitive-style accessories continue to surface to make it worth a visit.

Road T(r)ips

Keep your eye on the calendar when you travel. Reservations can become a necessity. Particularly if you're planning a trip during prom season, wedding season, or any other hotel-intensive regional event. Many towns and cities have limited hotel space. Plan ahead, even if you're only thinking of an exit ramp motel off the nearest interstate during peak local event seasons.

If you decide to make a weekend of it, call the local Chamber of Commerce or the Visitor's Center in the city closest to your destination. If you're unfamiliar with local Visitor's Centers, you'll be pleasantly surprised at what a gold mine of well-organized information these groups can be when it comes to hotels, motels, bed and breakfasts, rental cars, restaurants, and local events. They can fax, mail, or talk you through your options if you're planning a trip to their city.

KENTUCKY

450-MILE OUTDOOR MARKET   *Annual*
U.S. Highway 127 starting in Covington, Kentucky
☎ (800) 225-TRIP
Mid-August

The world's longest outdoor sale. People who live along the route, businesses, and state residents are invited to set up shop along U.S. Highway 127 to sell their "treasures." The only rule for the "dealers" is no used clothing. What's left are more than enough collectibles, musical instruments, and furniture to attract over 80,000 people in at least 35,000 cars.

The sale route is all along U.S. Highway 127 from Covington, Kentucky, to Chattanooga, Tennessee. In Chattanooga, take U.S. Highway 27 to Martin Luther King Boulevard, go two blocks east to Broad Street, turn right on Broad, and follow it to Lookout Mountain. Turn left on Tennessee Avenue and follow signs for Lookout Mountain Parkway (Highway 58) to Highway 157 South/Georgia, Highway 176 South/Alabama. You'll find plenty of other scenic attractions and events along the way.

Louisville

KENTUCKY FLEA MARKET
Fairgrounds
☎ (502) 456-2244
Fri.–Sun.

This is a remarkably popular "mixed" market—especially over the New Year's holiday, when they host an extravaganza event. They've got more than their fair share of wholesale, discount merchandise, but what attracts decorators is the relatively small antique section that has a way of turning up the occasional Southern eccentricity as well as horse race motif wooden pocketbooks and some older pieces.

LOUISIANA

New Orleans

JEFF INDOOR FLEA MARKET   *Antique Mall*
5501 Jefferson Highway
☎ (504) 734-0087
Fri.–Sun. 10 A.M.–6 P.M.

Unlike the flea section of the French Quarter market, which mainly deals in souvenirs and Taiwanese imports, the Jeff Indoor Market is a cavernous 60,000 square-foot indoor facility packed with the usual range of Southern antiques and memorabilia. The goods to watch for include Depression glass, advertising ephemera, furniture leftovers from most of the twentieth century, 1950s kitchenware, chromeware, and brass-bladed fans. There is a snack bar—and best of all, air-conditioning.

Shreveport

THE ANTIQUE MALL
Antique Mall
546 Olive Street
☎ (318) 425-8786
Tues.–Sat. 10 A.M.–5 P.M.

If you're in the market for decorative antiques with an international upscale provenance, tour all 12,000 air-conditioned square feet of this downtown antique mall. The Antique Mall specializes in English, German, and French antiques and furniture from the eighteenth and nineteenth centuries.

There are also souvenirs to be had from the twentieth century. These include all sorts of art pottery like Roseville, the occasional Italian Murano glass find, 1950s lamps, and housewares from the last ten decades. Don't expect to stockpile linens; they tend to be in short supply.

One word of warning: this antique mall doesn't take credit cards.

MARYLAND

Crumpton

DIXON'S AUCTION AND FLEA MARKET
Junction of Rt. 443 and Rt. 290
Seventy-five miles from Washington, D.C.

☎ (301) 928-3006

Fifty-one Wednesdays a year

The flea market itself is held inside a cavernous barn and is nothing unusually special, but the Wednesday auctions are entirely another kettle of fish. This is the kind of place where other dealers buy up whole lots—just so they can host their own auctions. It's an action-packed, idiosyncratic outdoor auction with an auctioneer in a golf cart scooting from "pile to pile, aisle to aisle."

Stand by the lot that interests you and eventually the auctioneer will chug by with a posse of buyers and dealers placing bids on everything from rusted air conditioners and plastic cafeteria trays to horsehair sofas.

The auction is held rain or shine, which could be great for your pocketbook. When it rains, auction prices, even on Heywood-Wakefield, are said to be *really* remarkable. "Be here with me at ten dollars."

MASSACHUSETTS

Chilmark

CHILMARK FLEA MARKET
Chilmark Community Church
Menemsha Cross Road
Wed. and Sat. 8:30 A.M.–2 P.M., in season

Early risers have the edge and parking is a problem, but from July through Labor day, the local Chilmark scene features at least sixty-five dealers with better furniture, kitchenware, appliances, glassware, and decorative accessories than you might imagine—although like any market of this size, what you see, while occasionally choice, is nonetheless sporadic. But at least you can usually count on seeing an intriguing bunch of shoppers.

Brimfield

BRIMFIELD   *Seasonal*
Route 20, Brimfield, Mass. (near Sturbridge)
☎ (413) 245-9556

From points south, take I-95 north to I-91 north into Hartford, CT. From Hartford take I-91 to Springfield, Mass. Take I-291 to I-190 (Mass. Pike). Mass Pike east to exit 8 at Palmer. After exit, turn right at first stoplight, turn left onto Rt. 20. Go six miles east to Brimfield.

During the course of a weekend, up to 50,000 junkers compete for the ultimate find. It doesn't get much bigger or wilder than Brimfield. Over 3,000 dealers occupy twenty farm fields of land. In fact, there is so much ground to cover that when crowds are allowed to enter at 4 A.M., they sprint madly in every direction, making an effort not to get in each other's way.

Brimfield is known for having more major collectibles in more categories than any other market. A partial list of possibilities includes furniture and collectibles from the late eighteenth, nineteenth, and twentieth centuries. You'll also find plenty of one-of-a-kind weird things, secondhand stuff—and of course, parking hell! If you can't make up your mind about an object, be sure and write down the table number and any other information you need to find it's location again—otherwise you won't have a snowball's chance.

If you don't want to drive, there are many day trip bus tours that leave from New York and Boston. And there is even one organized by the Smithsonian that leaves from Washington led by a doyenne!

Absolutely, Brimfield will reward you—if you're long on ingenuity and perseverance. But only you know whether you're psyched enough to fight for a motel room, sit in traffic jams, hike the last mile after you've parked your car, and wait at least an hour for dinner at most of the local restaurants.

Serious Brimfield junkers pack two pairs of shoes and socks and switch them every six hours. But even those who are going just for a once-in-a-lifetime experience should remember to always bring their own bags, or at least one large tote bag. (As well as plenty of small bills and change.)

This market is a big deal. So get out the calendar and mark Brimfield as follows: six days, starting on the Tuesday *before* the second full weekends in May, July, and September.

Wellfleet

WELLFLEET DRIVE-IN FLEA MARKET
Route 6, Wellfleet Drive-In Theater
☎ (508) 349-2520

Sat.–Sun. 8 A.M.–4 P.M., April–October

It's neither exceptionally big nor famous, but if you're in Cape Cod, then the Wellfleet Drive-In is the place to be. It's got a playground for children and a friendly local scene with the occasional celebrity. More like a gregarious garage sale/craft fair/farmer's market than a major collectible scene but with enough surprising finds to keep regulars coming back. It's *exceptionally* erratic—with antiques and collectibles one week and predominantly new and discount goods the next. It all depends on which dealers show up that week.

MINNESOTA

THE 85-MILE GARAGE SALE   *Annual*

Held along Mississippi River on the banks of southeast Minnesota
    and southwest Wisconsin in Bluff County

☎ (800) 369-4123

Held annually in early May

This sprawling garage sale is held one weekend a year (call the Lake City Chamber of Commerce for exact dates). And if little else, when the weather is good, it's great outdoor fun. To get there, fly into the Minneapolis airport, rent a car, and drive an hour and half south. Maps of the route are available almost anywhere on the way. Stop anywhere where you see a clump of sales in any one block or when you see a large church rummage sign. Have lunch outside at an old-fashioned root beer stand, or enjoy a slice a pie from one of the neighborhood "dealers."

The pickings are garage sale basics. Lots of oddball stuff, children's clothes, and semi-antiquated appliances. You may have better luck at one of the many antique stores along the way, so think of it as a great scenic lark and a chance to explore the beautiful Minnesota countryside and antique shops.

Rochester

THE ORIGINAL GOLDRUSH
Olmstead County Fairgrounds
☎ (507) 356-4461
Second weekend of May and third weekend of August,
  sunrise to sunset

This one qualifies as both a humdinger and a hoot. (Midwest dealers swear it's "the place to go—and the place to be.") The Goldrush is held inside, outside, and all over a sprawling fairground venue. It's known for having quite a range of merchandise from wind-up toys, bad neon root beer signs, every salt and pepper shaker ever made, '50s appliances, aprons, and linens to vintage clothes, oak furniture, '50s furniture of no particular provenance, and one-of-a-kind pieces that might have come out of an old lodge hall or remodeled restaurant.

NEVADA

Las Vegas

In alter-economy circles, Las Vegas is known for its many pawn shops, stores that specialize in good luck objects with every metaphysical bent imaginable, and its gambling collectibles. It's also known for the Liberace Museum, which sells Las Vegas–style collectibles like ashtrays, should you have any room in your suitcase after stocking up on vintage poker chips, green felt remnants, and well-used dice.

THE HOUSE OF ANTIQUE SLOTS
Antique Boutique
1243 Las Vegas Boulevard
☎ (703) 382-1520

If you collect vintage slot machines, chances are you already know about this place. If not, don't expect to find a deal. Classic slot machines are around $2,000 and the prices go up from there. But hey, at least you can get your quarters back.

STONEY'S LOAN AND JEWELRY
Pawn Shop
126 South 1st Street
☎ (702) 384-0819

This is the oldest pawn shop in Las Vegas—and still a classic filled with watches, cameras, gold jewelry, television sets, and golf clubs. It's a great place to get lucky if you're in a buying mood.

NEW JERSEY

THE ATLANTIQUE CITY GALA
Atlantic City Convention Center
☎ (800) 526-2724
Held twice a year, call for annual dates

This is quite an event—attracting many shoppers with no qualms about putting themselves up at Trump Hotel and Casino the night before it opens just so they can get an early start. The Atlantique City Gala is sponsored by Brimfield Associates, and billed as "the largest indoor antique and collectible fair in the world." Don't let the indoor venue fool you. Inside the convention center you'll find 7½ acres of Kennedy memorabilia, industrial design furniture classics, formal and country furniture, automobilia, cowboy and Indian stuff, model cars, all kinds of train sets, ship and plane collectibles, handbags, fountain pens, vintage textiles, decorative accessories, china classics, art pottery, glass from the entire twentieth century, and gambling collectibles. And that's just to name a few of the categories this market is known for.

NEW MEXICO

Albuquerque

OPEN AIR FLEA MARKET
State Fairgrounds I-40, Louisiana Street and Central Street
☎ (505) 265-1791 or (505) 255-8255
Sat.–Sun.

Albuquerque is a blue-collar town that boomed during the '60s and '70s. Look for interesting twentieth-century fare at this forty-acre fairground market. Over two hundred dealers offer everything from beanbag chairs to handblown Chemex coffee makers, Venini glass, well-used hand tools, electric tools, Native American art, jewelry, and big, weird things. However, don't be surprised to see quite a lot of brand new discounted merchandise.

Since it's held on the fairgrounds, the Open Air Flea Market is closed annually for fair time in September.

Santa Fe

Franchise stores have made shopping a déjà vu experience no matter what city or state you're in, but regional markets like Trader Jack's demonstrate the extraordinary regional diversity in goods still available at flea markets.

People who have traveled the world live in Santa Fe. So does the past. This is a region that was fought over by the Spanish, the Mexicans, the Native Americans, and of course, Anglo cowboys. The descendants of all those people still live in Santa Fe, and few places capture their combined ethos more vividly than the eclectic bazaar that is Trader Jack's Flea market.

TRADER JACK'S FLEA MARKET   *Nine Months a Year*
Cerillos Road and Truck Bypass
☎ (505) 455-7874
Fri.–Sun. 8 A.M.–4 P.M.

Mountains loom in the distance and flute music drifts on pinion smoke. At this market, Tibetan and Balinese relics brought back by "hippies," Mexican relics, Pueblo Indian crafts, and all kinds of ethnic spiritual beads fill the tables.

That's only the beginning, though. Expect well-worn western gear and artifacts, leather tack, ceramic tile outdoor furniture, pine benches, bent willow chairs, southwestern pottery, silver jewelry (at exceptional prices), belts and buckles, African tribal artifacts, sepia photographs, carved wood santos statues, and hippie artifacts with an American early '60s provenance. (Plus, an extensive collection of western art from artists between galleries.) Try to get there by 9 A.M.; it can get so warm in the afternoons that many vendors begin packing up by 3:30 P.M.

THE SUMMER ANTIQUITIES SHOW
The Sweeney Center
Corner of Grant and Marcy
1½ blocks northwest of the Plaza
☎ (505) 984-6760

This is a summer high-end market for pre-1950 Native American, ethnographic, devotional, and pre-1960 western folk art. Even if you can't afford to invest heavily in this arena of American history, the Summer Antiquity Show also features a series of seminars on beadwork, blanket stripes, and tribal objects by experts that could be worth the investment if you're just entering the field.

The circuit for this market also includes Los Angeles, San Francisco, and San Rafael, California, as well as New York City and Chicago.

Let Your Fingers Do the Groundwork

Never be hesitant to call and ask questions—especially if you have to go out of your way to get there. Most markets, antique shows, and events have a telephone number for the public and dealers to get information and directions.

While there are currently at least 3,000 flea markets in the United States alone, you'll rapidly discover that not very many of them are known for antiques and collectibles. Many of them are little more than acre after dusty acre of brand-new, discounted, and handmade merchandise, and even live animals. If the prospect of driving a distance to end up looking at acres of tube socks makes you squeamish, it should motivate you to do your research ahead of time.

When you call, don't just ask questions, but probe for details, too. If you're told the market has a farmer's market and a flea market, always ask *what percentage* of the market is "antiques and collectibles" as compared to the percentage of discounted new stuff. Find out how many dealers will be there. Over a hundred dealers is usually a good sign the market is worth your while, particularly if it's a mixed market. And always ask what kind of admission fees are charged for each day of the market. Sometimes they are substantially higher on "dealer days."

It's also a good idea to ask how many of their dealers are *regular* dealers (who are there every week or month). At monthly markets a ratio of 75 percent regulars to 25 percent transient is considered excellent. Go for it.

NEW YORK

Bouckville

MADISON-BOUCKVILLE MARKET
Fifteen miles east of Syracuse on Route 20
Third weekend in August

En route from Syracuse to this annual market you'll drive past yard sale after yard sale as local residents and even some dealers line the road. Hold out for the main event and you'll find over 1,000 dealers from all over the United States and Canada converging in this antique-friendly town to set up tables under circus tents in the open fields.

Bouckville has gradually become a diamonds-in-the-rough flea mecca. It's an unpretentious, fun event that attracts all kinds of collectors and shop owners. Look for old farm furniture, moonshine jugs, and soda bottles as well as an occasional European antique, oriental rug, piece of estate jewelry, and silver find—in addition to all sorts of 1950s collectibles from Depression glass to ouiji boards. On the whole, upstate New York prices tend to be friendly and so do the people. The local Grange handles the food, several wandering barbershop quartets serenade junkers, and the local kids will help you carry your new purchases back to your car; and parking is free.

Hudson

Upstate New York is known for having some of the best-priced small town antique shops in the country. Hudson, while one of the most expensive of those towns, has nevertheless become one of the most popular of the upstate towns in flea aesthetic circles. (Manhattanites can take the Hudson line from Grand Central Station to get there.)

Some ten years ago a wide range of antique and "junque" dealers began taking over Warren Street; now there are forty shops along this strip with more opening all the time. Most specialize in nineteenth- and twentieth-century furniture, iron and stone garden furniture, antique cameras, and taxidermied dioramas. And if collecting Renaissance, Medieval, Heraldic, or Gothic is your grail, then you'll probably want to take a scenic trip upstate. Almost every shop has its own specialty, so plan to spend the day.

Hudson is a wonderfully austere, ungentrified New England Gothic storefront sort of town and the Victorian houses on the outskirts are equally picturesque. (But be careful where you park your car; regular Hudson enthusiasts report an occasional crime problem.)

20TH CENTURY   *Antique Boutique*
551 Warren Street (upstairs)

Owner Frank Rosa deals in well-made, beautiful furniture without concern for a name brand designer. It's a strategy that has helped him amass twentieth-century greats one step ahead of the crowd, from T. Robbs-Gibbing to McCobb wall units and bureaus to true 1950s atomic-lined classics whose names we may never be able to pinpoint. Don't miss his low-end oversized glass chemistry beakers.

THERON WARE   *Antique Boutique*
548 Warren Street

Not quite as drop-dead dramatic as some of its neighbors across the street, but you'll find yourself thinking about its well-worn leather club chairs, Pittsburgh glass, and small oil paintings for quite a while.

New York City

New York's secondhand and consignment shops thrill international designers and stylists the world over because Manhattan and its outer boroughs host some of the most fascinating junk stores, vintage clothes boutiques, and pawn shops in the world. Every weekend New York City hosts the Madison Avenue of flea markets—known as the 26th Street Flea Markets. But it's hardly the only alternative venue in this bustling city. The alter-economy is alive and well in every borough. Stoop shopping in Brooklyn has even become the urban equivalent of yard sales.

But Manhattanites don't even have to leave their house to buy used clothes and whatnots. There is even a local public access home shopping show called Alan & Suzi on Channel 35 on Mondays at 9 P.M., featuring some glamorous transvestite models selling designer clothes from the '70s and '80s.

Start with the venues listed below or choose your neighborhood and flip through the Yellow Pages.

ANNEX ANTIQUES FAIR AND FLEA MARKET (A.K.A. THE 26TH STREET MARKET) & THE GARAGE

(at 26th Street and 6th Avenue)

☎ (212) 243-5343

$1 admission fee to the main lot; surrounding lots are free

Some say it's got too much small stuff and not enough furniture. (A situation which can change dramatically in the summer.) Others gripe the prices aren't always the best. However, the 26th Street Market is informally thought to be the source of almost 60 percent of the goods that end up in the hippest "new antique stores" in SoHo—marked up considerably.

Serious shoppers and furniture enthusiasts show up at 6 A.M. The vogueing crowd starts arriving around 4 P.M. (Celebrity spotting includes supermodels, soap opera stars, and designers like Christian Lacroix, Todd Oldham, and Anna Sui.) Better yet, the outdoor market at 26th Street is the epicenter of the sprawling Annex empire—you'll find more markets indoors and out on all sides of the Annex.

Ask any local for directions to The Garage, a block away, or grab one of the flyers handed out along the perimeter. This underground parking-lot-turned-flea-market is a weekend source for vintage eyeglasses, Russel Wright this and that, strange bolts of fabric, Oriental antiquities, and all sorts of twentieth-century kitsch. Some snipe it's called The Garage because the selection is like a garage sale. If so, on a good day it's quite a heady Manhattan-style garage sale.

THE 26TH STREET INDOOR ANTIQUE FAIR
40 W. 25th Street (Broadway and 6th Avenue)
☎ (212) 633-6010
Sat.–Sun. 8:30 A.M.–5:30 P.M.

This is much like going to a weekly pier show with over one hundred reasonably high-end dealers inside this two-story indoor weekend market—complete with an espresso bar downstairs. Look for Art Deco, Judaica, silver candelabras, tea sets, toys, antique furniture, rare books, and vintage fountain pens, as well as all kinds of upscale nineteenth- and twentieth-century *objets,* from used designer clothing to French and American art and gallery exhibit posters. Prices are frequently higher than at some of the other nearby markets, and dealers frequently look irritated at the prospect of bargaining—still, unlike most antique malls staffed by a single cashier, this upscale antique mall has dealers who can answer detailed questions.

(International shoppers may be reminded of the antique section of Camden Passage in London. Expect a well-edited, sophisticated selection—at a price.)

THE I.S. 44 FLEA MARKET   *Weekly*
Columbus Avenue between 76th and 77th streets
☎ (212) 721-0900
Sun. 11 A.M.–5 P.M.

At first glance you may have your doubts. From the outside, this weekend schoolyard event looks to have nothing but standard discounted new merchandise like handmade crafts, tube socks, and vintage clothes. Inside is a different story.

I.S. 44 is known for its vintage costume jewelry, antiques, linens, and other houseware collectibles, which can be found inside the school's lobby as well as in the classrooms. Small as it is, you'll usually encounter a wide variety of inexpensive "smalls" from railroad linens and Masonic Temple greeting cards to vintage Arnold Palmer alpaca golf sweaters.

NORTH CAROLINA

Charlotte

The creation of a new football team and a whole influx of sports-loving residents may change collecting trends in this city—but don't count on it. Odds are, the new residents will also be collecting Regency wicker, Staffordshire pottery, oriental rugs, silver, and vintage garden statues.

METROLINA EXPO
7100 Statesville Road
☎ (704) 596-4643

The first weekend of every month, this sprawling monster market is reserved for antiques and collectibles. The first Thursday of the first weekend is earmarked as an early buyers day, Friday is supposed to be for shop owners and dealers—although no one checks for identification—and Saturdays and Sundays are open to the general public.

When you enter Metrolina, you'll walk directly into a very large building filled with nineteenth- and twentieth-century antiques and junk. The space looks so cavernous that you're likely to think it's the whole enchilada. It's not. So be sure and budget your time so you can meander around the many lots outside of the main structure. Some are dedicated to a single collectible like vintage fabrics and clothing or garden furniture, while others deal in a broad range of twentieth-century ephemera and clutter.

There are few true bargains to be had—they take vintage goods quite seriously in the South—but on the other hand, you will find an extraordinary amount of silver, stoneware, transferware, early tobacco tins, Majollica, and tack. And lately you'll find more and more mid-century coups like sports collectibles, lawn chairs from the 1940s, well-used garden tools, garden statuary, vintage clothing, and almost every colored Depression glass pattern imaginable. But by and large this market is dedicated to what's left of the late nineteenth century and early twentieth century.

(The second weekend is for crafts, and the third weekend of the month is set aside for a combination farmer's market/discount merchandise/"garage goods" sale.)

INTERIORS MARKETPLACE   *Antique Mall*
2000 South Boulevard
☎ (704) 377-6226
Mon.–Sat. 10 A.M.–6 P.M., Sun. 1 P.M.–5 P.M.

Their slogan is "where nothing is run of the mill." No surprise, since this popular downtown antique mall was a former mill before it was carefully renovated. And if you are the kind of shopper who still needs a little more ambiance and editing than you're likely to find at the nearby Metrolina Antique and Collectible Market, then this antique mall consisting of seventy-five mini-showrooms is for you. It's not cutting-edge antique chic in sensibility, but a wide range of dealers in upscale furniture, accessories, and vintage linens have all set up shop here. You'll find vintage decorative accessories with a distinctly Southern sensibility—which if you don't know by now is practically code for goods with an Italian, English, French, or Civil War provenance.

OHIO

A lot of people swear by Ohio flea markets due to the predominance of big houses, small towns, and deep heartland roots. The sheer volume of flea markets, auctions, and antique malls—many of which are considered source markets for everything from secret society artifacts to primitive pine furniture, skews the odds in your favor.

Zanesville

THE AMERICAN ART POTTERY SHOW   *Annual*
Pritchard/Laughlin Civic Center
Exit 176 off I-70

Between Zanesille and Cambridge Route 40
Third weekend of July

Because of its rich deposits of coal, fire clay, and natural gas, Zanesville is the historic home of Roseville and some forty other celebrated potteries like McCoy, Brush, Hull, and Shawnee. This annual market is a cross between a birthday bash, a convention of pottery lovers, and one heck of a market. Collectors, dealers, and shop owners from all over the country fly in to bargain for Roseville, Hull, Weller, Catalina, McCoy, early salt glaze, spongeware, and just about every other genre of American pottery from some seventy-five specialists.

The actual show is the culmination of a whole week of activities that includes a grand parade, a pageant and pie baking contest—as well as special meetings and seminars. (Plan to book your hotel room at least a year ahead.)

OKLAHOMA

Oklahoma has great flea markets with a lot of eccentric, unexpected industrial collectibles from vintage hair salons, diners, and who knows what else. You won't be disappointed.

Tulsa

TULSA STATE FAIRGROUNDS
21st and Yale
☎ (918) 744-1113
Saturday 7 A.M.–6 P.M.

This indoor market is spread throughout two very large buildings. Local artists show southwestern style here and you can even find artisans who specialize in custom woodworking. But the big attraction is the great range of one-of-a-kind goods. You'll encounter more than a little kitsch, traditional antiques, and southwestern collectibles as well as a lot of furniture from the '50s and '60s, jewelry, and silver, in addition to industrial finds like dark-green sparkling vinyl reclining chairs made for 1950s hair salons, diner stools, and a great deal more.

THE ADMIRAL FLEA MARKET
Admiral and Mingo
☎ (918) 936-1386
Fri.–Sun.

The area around this popular Oklahoma market is known for vintage clothing stores—and this market shares the town's enthusiasm. Admiral is an outdoor market that covers ten acres with big furniture, small furniture, household goods, Native American collectibles, secondhand garage goods, and all kinds of small collectibles as well as new merchandise, crafts, and clothes. However, they're particularly known for '60s finds since several dealers specialize in groovy psychedelic era furniture, plastic fantastic chairs, hip coffee tables, Lucite anything, and yellow smiley-face stuff.

OREGON

Once known merely as a great market for Pacific Northwest, Native American, and Eskimo artifacts, Oregon is a now the

Pacific wonderland for far more modern collections. Dealers run classifieds daily in search of vintage Levis, Hawaiian shirts, and military jackets. Vintage Nike sneakers can sell for hundreds if not thousands of dollars.

If you're in Oregon, always explore the church and charity thrift shops, especially the "as is" bins and departments— they can be a source of unusual finds from underwear to furniture.

Portland

PAY & PAK *Antique Mall*
8900 North Vancouver Avenue
☎ (503) 283-2940

Don't let the name mislead you. Once a handyman's store, Pay & Pak is now a popular indoor antique and collectible market packed with jewelry, musical instruments from ukuleles to violins, books, cameras, rare finds like a collapsible English paratrooper bicycle, and the occasional Cowboy or Native American collectible.

They also host a series of specialty shows annually, featuring vintage military goods like insignia and bayonets, toys like windups and Hotwheels, western relics, and western antique paper collectibles like postcards and prints.

THE EXPOSITION CENTER
2060 North Marine Drive
☎ (503) 282-0877

Seasonal; call for dates

Three times a year, Palmer, Wirfs & Associates host huge antique shows with upward from 1,500 dealers specializing in all sorts of Arts and Crafts, furniture, books, estate jewelry, Art Deco, Depression glass, art pottery, Native American art, vintage cowboy shirts, and popular local collectibles like Coon Chicken Inn restaurant ware.

This event has become so popular you need to park somewhere else and hop a shuttle bus to the Expo Center.

THE PORTLAND SATURDAY MARKET
Under the west end of the Burnside Bridge
☎ (503) 222-6072

This crafts market started in the legendary hippie depths of Eugene, Oregon, and is now a Portland institution. Don't go for the collectibles. Stop by because in addition to being a showcase for all sorts of local artists, it's a crowded enthusiastic scene complete with street musicians. Occasionally a dealer of vintage goods even sets up a table. This market is held every Saturday from the first weekend in March though Christmas Eve.

PENNSYLVANIA

Pennsylvania is a hotbed of American collectibles specialties like painted wood-grain furniture. It's also a great scene for antiques in general, thanks to a large and knowledgeable dealer population. The state boasts Antique Row, a noteworthy stretch along Route 272 of some five hundred-plus dealers offering antiques and collectibles every weekend. All of them advertise free parking and free admission. You'll be shoulder to shoulder with trendy New York dealers looking for the next great thing, so if you need pointers, just eavesdrop.

Adamstown

THE BLACK ANGUS ANTIQUE MARKET
Route 272, exit 21
☎ (215) 484-4385
Sunday 8 A.M.–5 P.M.

This is a legendary antique mall on Rt. 272—which is saying a lot—given the increasingly competitive nature of antique markets on this famous strip. Black Angus is a spacious, atmospheric market in the midst of a sort of polka dance hall/beer brewery complex. Up to 250 experienced, knowledgeable dealers sell a wide range of one-of-a-kind antiques and collectibles. Look for fountain pens, medical and pharmaceutical wonders, small oil paintings, unusual lamps, upscale costume jewelry, cowboy this and that, dark wood furniture, the occasional early electronic find, as well as silver candlesticks, and tea sets galore.

RENNINGER'S ANTIQUE MARKET 1
Route 272, ½ mile north of Pennsylvania Turnpike, exit 21
☎ (717) 385-0104
7:30 A.M.–5 P.M.

"Antiques and collectibles only" is the management rule at this year-round rambling indoor-outdoor Sunday market.

Renninger's is known for curious finds—and lots of them. In fact, many decorators and store owners with pricey Manhattan boutiques consider this rustic maze-like market a rich source of goods they can later resell.

A little of everything is at Renninger's. Dark, somewhat musty indoor aisles are packed with vintage textiles, Cambridge flash glass, art pottery like yellow and brown Jaska, volumes of vintage leather books, and quite a mix of twentieth-century furniture from wicker to Hoosier. It's also got a lot of children's collectibles like vintage wind-up toys, globes, model airplane kits, and who knows what else. The sheer volume of small goods tucked away in crevices is fascinating—although the prices can be higher than you might expect.

(In the summer, the outdoor tables close up early in the afternoon, so try to begin outside at the area furthest from the shade of the trees and then work your way indoors.)

Kutztown

RENNINGER'S ANTIQUE MARKET 2
740 Noble Street, one mile south from the middle of town
☎ (717) 385-0108
Fri. 12 P.M.–8 P.M., Sat. 8 A.M.–5 P.M.

This combination farmer's market/new merchandise/antiques indoor market is usually worth exploring—and not just for Amish furniture and quilts. Valuable toys consistently turn up here, so do strange one-of-a-kinds. (Not to be confused with the seasonal—and fabled—Renninger's Extravaganza also held here at the Kutztown location.) The spread of antique malls in Pennsylvania also means that there are now far more locations for local dealers to choose from so the mix and the magic can vary.

RENNINGER'S EXTRAVAGANZA
Noble Street, one mile south from the middle of town
☎ (717) 336-2177

A favorite among stylists and store owners from all over the map for the sheer volume displayed by 1,200 dealers. The Extravaganza is an antiques and collectibles–only market known for curious finds and occasionally even great prices. Renninger's Extravaganza is second only to Brimfield in fame—and it's easier to navigate. This is one of those legendary seasonal markets that are great fun and an increasingly great scene. In addition to twentieth-century finds, it's also known for having big stuff like bathtubs, canoes, etc.

Held Thursday, Friday, and Saturday of the last full weekends of April, June, and September. Special antiques and collectibles shows are held the third weekend of every month 9 A.M.–5 P.M.

Getting the Stuff Home

If you're looking for furniture in out-of-the-way flea markets, rent a van or a truck for the return trip. Bring blankets and padding to protect any glass or furniture buys as you transport them home.

If you've purchased small goods out of town and you don't want to carry them home personally, use a private mailing service to wrap, crate, and ship them for you. Just flip through the local Yellow Pages to find the closest UPS drop-off or storefront pack-and-ship. Keep in mind that many small mailers will only handle dimensions up to 30" x 26" x 24". Plus, most pack-and-ship services use UPS, and they will only handle up to seventy pounds per package.

But don't despair, you can get nearly anything home if you put your mind to it, and most dealers will be glad to help you brainstorm! (Occasionally, since dealers travel on a circuit, it's even possible to find a dealer who will carry your furniture purchase in their van until they reach a more convenient city for you to pick it up in.)

Auction houses will usually deliver for a fee or at least give you the name of a man with a truck. Many pier shows offer shipping and delivery services for a fee. You can usually arrange for a mover to pick up your goods from a thrift shop or a tag sale if they don't fit in your car. (If you need to have your goods insured, be sure to use a professional mover.)

SOUTH CAROLINA

Charleston

Charleston is a chic port city known for its sleek sophistica-tion, the Spoleto art festival, and its unusually cosmopolitan antique shopping. King Street in particular is known as a nonstop boulevard of dreams for chic antiques and unusual decorative accents. However, local residents who aren't desperate for authenticated Adams, Regency, Duncan Phyfe, and Queen Anne furniture often head out of town to find the kind of secondhand budget-price mohair club chairs they can slipcover, wicker they can spray paint, and antique pole fans to cut the summer heat.

THE LOW COUNTRY FLEA MARKET AND COLLECTIBLES SHOW
77 Calhoun (in the Gaillard Auditorium)
☎ (803) 884-7204
Third weekend of every month

Lately, Charleston has become the destination of choice among sophisticated travelers and not just during the Spoleto art festival either. If you find yourself there on the third weekend of the month, make it a point to stop by this popular local event.

It features antiques and collectibles with an emphasis on "upscale goods" (as opposed to kitsch). Finds like Georgian silver, decorative accessories, Staffordshire porcelains, fine jewelry, old prints, and a wide selection of toys seem to be on the minds of many shoppers and local dealers who know what they're looking for. Local antique shop owners consider the Low Country Flea Market and Collectibles Show a "source market"—which doesn't mean the prices are exceptional, but it does mean there is a constant source of interesting goods.

HUNGRYNECK ANTIQUE MALL   *Antique Mall*

401 Johnnie Dodds Boulevard

☎ (803) 849-1744

Mon.–Sat. 10 A.M.–6 P.M., Sun. 1 P.M.–5 P.M.

This quiet antique mall on the outskirts of Charleston is a well-guarded secret among local shopkeepers. It's known for turning up unusual pieces fairly regularly. There's not much furniture; however, you can anticipate decorative accessories and housewares like intricate ships under glass, stone garden statuary, Fiesta pieces, great prices on Stangel pots, strange boxes, silver this and that, and vintage linens. And even though it's indoors, you'll discover Hungryneck has even managed to replicate the dust and pollen of an outdoor market.

Finding your way to Johnnie Dodds Boulevard from downtown can be tricky. If you're new to the area, get a local resident to draw you a map or let you follow them there.

PAGES THIEVES MARKET   *Antique Mall*

1460 Ben Sawyer Boulevard

☎ (803) 884-9672

Mon.–Sat. 9 A.M.–6 P.M.

You'll know you're there when you spot the huge off-kilter clock out front. While deservedly popular with the in-the-know set, this antique-filled barn is hardly as glam as the contemporary antique shops of Charleston's fabled King Street, which may be why it's a local favorite of thrifty Martha Stewart–style fixer-upper fans.

Furniture mavens like it because it's packed all the way to the high-ceilinged wooden rafters with early, dark wood furniture, light pine furniture that works with Charleston's many urban ocean views, mohair-covered armchairs ready to be slipcovered, Formica tables from the '50s, wicker body baskets once used by undertakers to transport bodies, antique pole fans, Depression glass, and an excellent vintage linen selection. It also has slightly more twentieth-century furniture finds than many of its King Street competitors.

TERRACE OAKS ANTIQUES MALL   *Antique Mall*
2037 Maybank Highway

Off downtown King Street, this tastefully quiet—some say too quiet—antique mall holds forty dealers who let you browse through roomlike settings of antiques and curious funk. Tortoiseshell boxes, screens, chandeliers, apothecary jars, sepia prints, chests, Civil War memorabilia, and nice furniture.

DECORATORS ALLEY   *Antique Boutique*
177½ King Street
☎ (803) 772-2707

If King Street antiques are not quite flea enough for your sensibilities, try this small upstairs store filled with twentieth-century bits and pieces like wrought iron, statuary, and occasional chairs from the '20s and '30s, late '50s furniture, and practically new antiques! It's friendly, fanciful, and occasionally even has excellent bargains on mid-century must-haves.

TENNESSEE

Memphis

MID-SOUTH COLISEUM
Fairgrounds, East Parkway and Southern Avenue
☎ (901) 276-3532
First, second, and fourth weekends except during fair time

A thirty-year-old tradition. Dealers converge from near and far to set up shop at this popular local market, which usually has all kinds of decorative accessories, furniture, mixing bowls, canisters, clothing, old calendars and advertising art, used sporting goods, and the occasional twentieth-century end-table, chair, or Formica table.

Nashville

NASHVILLE FAIRGROUNDS FLEA MARKET
Tennessee State Fairgrounds
South of downtown Nashville
☎ (615) 383-7636
Last weekend of the month (except September and December)

Don't expect to park anywhere nearby, but do expect a little of everything else at this huge, colorful, indoor-outdoor market known as a "source market" among dealers and shop-keepers—which is a giveaway for the presence of "real antiques." Look for Americana, silver this and that, cut glass, and classic southern specialties like Depression glass, Coca-Cola, cigarette, and advertising collectibles, and of course, garden statues, benches, and lawn chairs. More mid-century stuff is slowly starting to turn up.

TEXAS

Unlike the South and the North, where houses were usually built with attics and basements—the better to store out-of-favor treasures—Texans built slab houses, with no attics and no basements.

What they brought with them was often used up or thrown out—which may be why a lot of the nineteenth- and twentieth-century goods you find in Texas tend to come from enterprising dealers on their way back from the Midwest. Even so, every so often you'll find goods that resonate real Texas, like made-in-Mexico pottery, wildcatter memorabilia, and vintage cowboy boots galore. However, keep in mind you'll pay more for cowboy and country memorabilia in the Southwest, where they are hot commodities.

San Antonio

Home of the legendary Alamo, where brave soldiers from all over the country and even the world died holding down the Fort. This is also a town where cattle once roamed free up and down every street.

Well, the Alamo is still standing—and selling an astounding range of memorabilia—however, the cows have moved on. San Antonio today is a thriving convention center, with a busy downtown antique and collectibles scene close enough to walk to from almost any hotel.

ALAMO ANTIQUE MALL   *Antique Mall*
125 Broadway
Daily 10 A.M.–6 P.M.

Not much furniture, but you'll find several floors of antiques, silver, and eclectic collectibles from Limoges and Roseville to used cowboy boots and juice glasses from just about every major gas and oil conglomerate.

HALF MOON   *Antique Mall*
112 Broadway Antiques
10 A.M.–6 P.M.

More like a great garage sale with a few unexpected Texas surprises, like a child's-size John Deere tractor, heavy glass paperweights from poultry shows, vintage cowboy boots, and utilitarian Mexican pottery. Treasures also include the occasional transferware breakfast set, cast metal toy soldiers, Murano glass, and silver candlesticks galore.

WYOMING

JACKSON HOLE WYOMING ANNUAL ELK ANTLER AUCTION
☎ (800) 443-6931
Usually held the third week in May; call the local Chamber of
  Commerce for details

There's nothing else like it. Anywhere.

Rumored to be the best source of antelope antlers and horn in the country, this annual auction features bighorn sheep, moose, and any other antler or horn collected by the Boy Scouts. Expect several thousand attendees, including Adirondack artists who incorporate antlers and bones in their art as well as many Japanese who bid for bones in quantity in order to grind them up for aphrodisiacs.

International Markets

CHAPTER 8

If you are traveling internationally and you want to get a real sense of the history and character of a place, browse an international flea market. It can be one of the most visually—and psychically—memorable experiences you will have abroad. Plus, it can also be one of your more economical experiences as well.

The alter-economy is everywhere, so never limit yourself to the tourist parts of town. Stop in at a church jumble or find a secondhand goods store to explore. They're not always in the best parts of town, but they're invariably a fascinating way to find bargains, see a rich cross section of the population, and get a sense of the cultural influences at play.

One word of caution: Be on your guard when you're at an international flea market. No matter where you go, whether it's Europe, Asia, or the Middle East, never pull out large wads of money. Carry small bills divided into many pockets so it looks as if you might be short of money when you do pull out your cash to pay.

And don't buy anything that is really old. Legal restrictions are important when you're shopping for antiques and every country has its own set of rules, seals, and tariffs. Call the embassy or customs about specific restrictions if you're in the market for antiquities—especially ones with religious overtones. In countries like Turkey they will have absolutely no qualms about arresting you for transporting prohibited artifacts. So be cautious about buying anything too antique. You never know how pricey or how uncomfortable a violation can be.

It should also go without saying that endangered materials like tortoiseshell combs will usually be confiscated by customs.

But there are so many extraordinary, evocative objects to be found at international flea markets that even if it's not an original mosque relic it will still be a miracle find wrapped in mystique—just because you had an adventure.

Tips for Travelers

☆ Even more than American markets, international markets use the asking price as a starting point. Except for some German markets, they really don't expect you to offer to pay the asking price. Really. (On the other hand, you probably won't do better than a 30 percent discount.)

♣ Your best bargaining ploys are to state what the cost is in American dollars—then say you would need to save at least 40 percent (for example) in order for you to afford a wonderful clock like that. Or ask if they will throw in something else. This is a particularly good strategy if you are buying more than two things; ask for a third to be included for the price of two.

✳ Dress casually. For your own protection never overdress in a way that shouts "rich American." You may even want to leave dramatic wedding rings and obviously expensive watches in the hotel safe. Notice how the local population dresses and try to blend in. If they're wearing blue jeans and a nice shirt, well, so should you.

✳ Numbers are a universal language, especially if you're a serious bargainer. Numbers work well with the well-known international language of smiles, grimaces, and hand signs. If you don't know the language, always bring a guide or a pad of paper. Have the vendor write down a price, consider it, and write down your best price. This could go on for a while. Anytime you feel like you're being taken, smile and simply walk away.

☆ There's no reason to be hostile if you think the price is too high. In most countries it's better to be indirect than rude. For example, being complimentary about a piece but blaming a third person who is far away yields much better results than a head-on collision, i.e., "It's wonderful but my wife would never let me pay this much."

✳ If you're not really interested in buying a piece—even at the price you've suggested—never waste the dealer's time engaging in a haggling session.

✳ If it's too big to carry home with you, you'll have to ship it. Be warned, international shipping can be more expensive than you might imagine. So even if it appears to be a great price on a pair of French beautifully distressed leather club chairs, don't forget to factor in the cost of getting them safely home. (Shipping two armchairs from Paris to New York, for example, is in the neighborhood of $800.) And the teakwood and wrought-iron garden set you found at a market in Thailand for a mere $300 will end up costing at least $1,000 to ship home. The big international markets like Cligancourt in Paris or Fairfield in England have shipping agents on the premises—otherwise ask a dealer to give you the name of a shipping agent to contact. In Asia, before you shop for anything you can't carry, check with the local American embassy about the best way to have it sent.

♣ Don't even think about requesting mailing or shipping if you're having trouble with the language barrier while you're negotiating. If you can carry it, bring it to the hotel with you and have the concierge advise you or check with the embassy. *Always try to pack it yourself* unless you're buying from quite a tony market. Otherwise, don't count on seeing it again. You may receive nothing or you might be mailed a different rug than the one you selected.

✳ Never trust *anyone* except a qualified shipping agent to mail anything for you. Horror stories abound. Find out how they plan to pack the goods, what form of transportation they will use, and how long it will take. Try to pay by credit card so you have some recourse if your crate doesn't show up in thirty days. (After that you won't be able to stop payment.)

☆ Fold down a sturdy cardboard box and pack it in your suitcase. Then you can fill it up and bring it back on the plane with you. Don't forget string and a handle.

♣ Federal Express and DHL have international and courier shipping services in European countries. Before you leave, you may want to get a list of their locations and any relevant regulations.

✱ Be sensible about carrying your money. Poverty in some countries is almost beyond imagination. Remember to only bring small denominations to a flea market. And *never* pull out your money except to make a purchase. Women should keep their wallet in the bottom of their purse, and keep their purse in front of them. Men should split their money between at least two pockets.

✳ If you're shopping abroad for furniture or accessories, know the exact dimensions of the rooms in your house. You might even want to pack photos of every room so you can get a sense of how it might look once you've gotten it home.

☆ Don't forget to be alert for furniture and trash-pickup days when you're in Europe. The money you save could offset the shipping charges.

AFRICA

Angola

ROQUE SANTERIA
Luanda

If you're a foreigner, then hire a police escort before you explore this rambling seaside bazaar that is Africa's largest flea market and scene.

You'll browse to the pulsing boom box beat of Brazilian sambas while you explore acres of booths selling an astounding mix of legal and illegal goods. These range from television sets, African glass bead or carved wood heirlooms, headless chickens, and witch doctor concoctions to penicillin, French perfume, and the occasional AK-47. If you don't see what you're looking for, make a few inquiries and odds are it will appear.

BELGIUM

Brussels

PLACE DU GRAND SABLON
Sat. 9 A.M.–6 P.M., Sun. 9 A.M.–2 P.M.

In back of the Notre Dame du Sablon, you'll find over ninety dealers selling European and Chinese porcelain, leather bound books, oil paintings, wall clocks, and all sorts of vintage silver flatware, candlesticks, kitchenwares, and objects meant for a mantelpiece.

BURMA

Unlike Thailand, where local currency is a must for flea market transactions, you can occasionally pay in American dollars in Burma. The government, however, prohibits the export of true religious and archeological antiquities.

Mandalay

ZEGYO MARKET
Huge lion gates usher you into this dark, almost medieval-feeling daily market. You won't find anything trendy but you will find food, sarongs, tree bark, meditation bells, and all kinds of everyday Burmese goods.

CANADA

Canada is known for its primitive pine furniture like great kitchen tables, hutches, and armoires. These items have appreciated in value considerably since American pickers started hauling away truckloads of remarkable pieces back across the border. But pine primitives are only half the story. Canada is also a consistently fascinating source of twentieth-century classics with an English provenance like Beswick and Alfred Reed Pottery, Carleton ware, and wildly colored '60s Dorset pottery—as well as used hockey sticks, snow shoes, and Royal commemoratives.

Toronto

HARBOURFRONT ANTIQUE MARKET
390 Queen's Quay West
☎ (416) 260-2626
Tues.–Fri. 11 A.M.–6 P.M., Sun. 8 A.M.–6 P.M.

If a movie is being filmed in Canada, chances are you will not only find the propmaster wandering through this two-story vintage wonderland overlooking the renovated harbourfront, but you'll also spot American movie stars from the cast on the prowl.

Toronto natives consider the prices here high, but the exchange rate makes many of the prices fairly reasonable for Americans. Another reason travelers come from all over to visit the Harbourfront Market is because the selection is amazing. Everything from 1940s black leatherette office chairs to Miss Piggy juice glasses and the exact match for practically every silver teaspoon ever made turns up here in quantity. It's also known for its typewriters, Persian antiques, Austrian crystal costume jewelry, antique Chinoiserie, well-known pottery, sporting goods—including silver plated cross-country and hockey trophies—transferware breakfast sets, estate wedding rings, and a great stock of English and art pottery from names like Beswick and Suzy Cooper.

Tip: If you're planning to bargain, bring American dollars.

CHINA

If you buy antiques in China, you will need to have a red seal affixed to each piece in order to bring them home with you. If the dealer doesn't have the proper seal, visit the Beijing Arts Objects Clearance Office situated in a compound of the Friendship Store. A small fee per piece is charged.

Most Chinese don't speak English, but don't fear; most store and stall owners do know enough English to conduct rudimentary haggling.

Beijing

JINGSONG MARKET (GENTLE PINES)
Sat. and Sun.

Ask the cabdriver to take you to Jingsong Market or get directions from your concierge—it's well known. Get there by 6

A.M. The place will be packed with Chinese, Germans, Swedes, English—and lately more and more Americans.

You'll know you're there when you see two rubble lots on either side of the street where houses have been pulled down. One side is "contemporary junk": old televisions, clothing, shoes, housewares.

But on the other side of the street is a little wall with all kinds of treasures lurking behind it. You'll see vintage books, bric-a-brac, clocks, Mao memorabilia, and kitsch from China and Russia. You'll even find many Tibetan dealers in full *llasa* with all sorts of Buddhist collectibles and mantra beads. Plus, there are antiquities, especially porcelain, brass, and carved wood things.

A candid Beijing cabdriver observed en route to Jingsong that if there is one thing the Chinese do well it's "make things look old." All you can do is bargain hard and hope for the best.

THE HONGQUIAO MARKET   *Daily*
Near the north gate of Tiantai

This isn't really a flea market. It's a street of nearly fifty antique shops where you can browse to your heart's content alongside diplomats, collectors, and Chinese dealers. Hongquiao is a must if you're searching for valuable snuff bottles, jade, ceramics, or contemporary pieces.

Young collectors from all over Asia are especially enamored of Hong Kong advertising art from the '50s and '60s. In particular, they gobble up the sort that resembles illustrated calendar art of movie stars with tasteful logos in the corner.

DENMARK
Copenhagen

LYNGBY
Sun. 8 A.M.–2 P.M.

The Lyngby Market is a short train ride from Copenhagen, and is a magnet for dealers from across the Scandinavian countries. Go if you're a fan of Danish teak furniture, any of the Scandinavian-designed furniture from the '50s and '60s, household goods, or vintage Scandinavian jewelry. Plus, the towns around Lyngby are known for historic homes that are open to the public and well worth visiting for ideas.

ENGLAND
London

BERMONDSEY
Bermondsey Street and Long Lane
South of Tower Bridge
4 A.M.–late afternoon

Bermondsey is best on Friday mornings. However, you need to keep a wary eye out for "artful reproductions." This shouldn't put you off since you'll have some five hundred stalls to explore in search of your heart's desire.

You'll see everything from antique tiles, silver candelabras, Staffordshire figurines, and Tiffany lamps to architectural tools and vintage golf clubs jumbled together. Oil paintings abound. If you're very lucky you'll spot a piece of Gothic revival furniture, an English Arts and Crafts piece, or a '60s clothing coup.

Be warned, like all outdoor London flea markets, the better the weather, the worse the crowds. This one opens up at 4 A.M., so if the weather threatens to be spectacular, pack a flashlight in your suitcase and beat the hordes.

PORTOBELLO ROAD
Sat. 5:30 A.M.–3 P.M.

When it comes to quality, the Portobello market has had its share of ups and downs. But when you do find vintage goods, expect countless retro-fashion-find shoes, fascinating clothes, stoneware teapots, enamelware teapots, milk jugs, fantastic tea sets, Victorian and contemporary jewelry, old games, medical and scientific instruments, treasures from India, all kinds of silver decorative accessories, and commemorative finds from coronations to weddings to centennials. (The "best" dealers set up near Ladbroke Grove.)

A lot of mid– and late–twentieth century finds that turn up are still undervalued in England. Look for '60s amorphous plastic wonders, ultra-cool British Hornsea ceramic pots, and wildly colored Dorset tableware.

ALFIES
13-25 Church Street
Tues.–Sat. 10 A.M.–6 P.M.

On Saturdays at the south end of this Church Street market, some three hundred dealers sell a wide variety of collectibles. Most of those dealers specialize in traditional Art Deco and Art Nouveau classics, although word has it more recent decades have gradually begun to surface.

Newark

THE NEWARK INTERNATIONAL ANTIQUES FAIR
The Newark and Nottingshire Showground
Off the A-1 (two hours' drive north of London), or take the train
   from London's Kings Cross station to Newark North Gate

The Newark International Antiques Fair is popular because it's big—and big because it's popular. Aisle after aisle are crammed with early twentieth-century English mailboxes, Georgian silver, tasteful garden statues, Arts and Crafts pottery, distinctive furniture, manufactured furniture, odd lamps, Scandinavian and Italian Glass, vintage European linens, storage jars, unusual furniture, Thai antiquities, vintage French housewares and decorative accessories, scientific curiosities, Victorian bric-a-brac, and more.

It's held two days (one for the trade and one for the public) in February, April, June, August, October, and December. At least 3,000 dealers from all over England and Europe make this event the Brimfield of Europe without the frazzle and frenzy.

The main line Newark station is connected with Eurolink providing trains and EuroStar service direct to and from London,

Paris, and Brussels. (If you need accommodations, there is a free service to assist you in finding a hotel.)

There is no currency exchange. Bring English pounds or pound traveler's checks, although major credit cards and U.S. cash are accepted. Several shippers have representatives stationed there. A wooden desk that measures roughly 52" x 30" x 30" should cost in the neighborhood of $350–$400 to ship—including insurance. Naturally, you should be able to carry small objects home in your luggage.

FRANCE

There are weekly markets all over France. To find out what events, flea markets, and fairs are going on throughout the country, be sure and get a copy of a free guide called L'incontournable du Chineur that is given out at almost any flea market. It will tell you what markets are scheduled throughout the Riviera and Provence.

Paris

PORTE DE CLIGANCOURT
Metro: Porte de Cligancourt
Sat.–Mon. 9:30 A.M.–6 P.M.

This is oldest and biggest market in Europe. There are almost twelve separate flea markets along the boundaries of this one market, each with its own name and specialty. There are over

1,600 merchants, including major antique dealers, minor antique dealers, and very humble dealers. Cligancourt is a nine-mile maze of passageways and streets like you wouldn't believe. Gems, jewels, and junk abound. Far more so than Portobello Road in London, Cligancourt is known as a furniture heaven. You'll find perfectly distressed leather club chairs, extraordinary armoires, astonishing coffee tables, one-of-a-kind beds, and evocative rolltop desks. You'll also see fascinating porcelains, prints, antique jewelry, ceramics, vintage clothing, hats, accessories, silver, fireplace tools, and more kitchen paraphernalia than even Julia Child herself might ever need.

Be sure and buy a copy of the *Guide Emer des Puces* ($5) which is sold at the market, or look for the free map. You'll need *some* sort of map to help you find the locations of automatic teller machines, toilets, taxi stands, and restaurants. The *Guide Emer des Puces* also tells you which dealers are known for what, how to use the shipping services, and where they are located.

MARCHE PAUL BERT/MARCHE SERPETTE
Saint Ouen
Rue des Rosier (or Rue Paul Bert)
Sat.–Mon. 7A.M.–7P.M.

These two Cligancourt markets are often a first stop for decorators and antique dealers. Along these stylish streets of antique stores known for quality, you'll find a stylish, pricey, and consistently fascinating assortment of chic wares.

Although lately the twentieth century is becoming a big draw, especially if you're looking for furniture classics like Knoll Saarinen or Jean Prouve, this market is a fast trip to the eighteenth and nineteenth centuries. One-of-a-kind garden furniture, turn-of-the-century landscapes, gothic mantelpieces, old but chic drafting tables, copper cookware, unframed nineteenth century portraits, kitchen goods, and a great deal more, *naturellement*.

PUCES DU MONTREUIL
Metro: Porte du Montreuil

Some French claim it's a trash and treasure classic. Others sneer at secondhand goods. In any event, don't let the plumbing and electrical supplies throw you. If you're at all obsessive, you'll probably turn up a little Baccarat something-or-other or at the very least a trés chic doorknob.

Vanves

PUCES DE VANVES
At Georges Lafenestre and Marc Sangrier avenues
Metro: Porte de Vanves
Sat. and Sun. 7 A.M.–7 P.M.

This two-block open-air market is reasonably easy to navigate and priced to move briskly. Vanves is especially known for having more than its fair share of French twentieth-century classic goods. Keep your eye out for mid-century gold jewelry, kitchenware, ceramics, dinnerware, leather-bound books, and hem-stitched linen sheets.

Provence

ISLE-SUR-LA-SORGUE
Sat. and Sun. 9 A.M.–7 P.M.

This legendary market is located at the far end of this lovely town, along the Sorgue riverbank's high street. Normally, it's a small weekend market which is open on Sundays (rare in Provence). However at Easter and the Assumption Day weekend in August, the whole town becomes a market with more than six hundred dealers selling lovely Provencal fabrics, d'Anduze pots, regional furniture, and all sorts of other art pottery, glassware, and quilts.

GERMANY

Berlin

KUNST UND NOSTALGIEMARKT
Grosser Berliner Kunst
Trodlmarket
Sat. and Sun. 10 A.M.–5 P.M.

This sprawling mixed market encompasses a crafts and secondhand section, a flea market, and an antique market. Each of which has a slightly different daily schedule although everyone is there on the weekend. Popular collectibles among local German shoppers include opera glasses, German ceramics, mechanical watches, and embroidered tablecloths.

WINTERFELDTMARKET
Winterfeldplatz
Wed. and Sat. 8 A.M.–1 P.M.

This is a very popular local market. Secondhand books, a lot of clothing, all sorts of plants, and many cafes nearby make it worth a stop.

ZILLE-HOF
Fasanenstrasse 14½
Mon.–Fri. 8:30 A.M.–5:30 P.M.

More like a great junk store and less like an antique market, Zille-Hof is a great place to look for European twentieth-century collectibles—including those no one else has started collecting quite yet. But be warned, the prices aren't cheap.

GARAGE
Ahornstrasse 2
Mon.–Sat. 12 P.M.–9 P.M.

Vintage and used clothing are one of the better buys in Germany, and the Garage is one of the largest secondhand clothing stores in Europe. Since you pay by the pound for the clothing you buy, it's hard to go wrong. This is the place to go if you're a fan of vintage military clothing. They also have a wide selection of trendier clothing.

INDIA

You may start to feel as if all of India is a metaphorical flea market, but shop carefully despite the low prices, especially if you're shopping for authentic antiques. Many pieces have been artificially aged, and India prohibits the export of anything over one hundred years old.

Haggling is an art form of such epic proportions in India that even years of shopping Brimfield scarcely prepares you to get anywhere near the dealer price. So why bother? Just do the best you can and remember to never walk directly toward the object your heart desires and shriek. But don't let it slip through your fingers for the sake of a few rupees either.

A concierge or a friend in Delhi can usually recommend a guide to go with you to either of the markets listed below. It's easy to get lost within markets. No matter where you go, be on the lookout for implements like bells, plates, lamps, and ladles used for rituals and family altars as well as icons, prayer shawls, and all sorts of brass.

Delhi

HAUZ KHAS VILLAGE

This new shopping site was once a cattle village—and you'll see and smell that heritage immediately. These days, however, Hauz Khas is a village of alleys, some new and chic, some less so. Haus Khas Village is not exactly a true flea market, but it is a great place to find a wide variety of antiques from the British Raj era, as well as Rajasthani puppets, brass, brocades and silk, and bronze images of deities.

SUNDER NAGAR MARKET

It's arduous indeed, but Sunder Nagar is one of the most famous brass and antique markets in all of India. This is a flea market of epic proportions—and equally epic dealers when it comes to the art of haggling. Browse endlessly for voluptuous vintage goods including lavish prayer shawls, heavy iron scrolled screens, statues of Hindu gods, miniature Mughal paintings, mosaic-topped tables, decorative silver, wool tribal rugs, intricate carved woods, as well as aged brass sconces, planters, pots, and *much* more.

INDONESIA

Bali

THE MARKET

The flea market doesn't really have an address in the traditional sense, but it's a small island, and any concierge will be able to direct you from your hotel.

Almost immediately you'll notice this tropical market is conveniently compartmentalized by sections. Aisles include active livestock as well as underwear, jellies, bamboo you-name-its, beetle nut boxes, livestock, teal salad bowls, and T-shirts. But for the careful eye there is also an antiquities section, where you'll find vintage spears, shields, and other war paraphernalia. For many Americans the real draws are the silver jewelry and toe rings.

Jakarta

THE OUTDOOR MARKET

Ask your concierge for directions from your hotel. But be warned, the hard-sell atmosphere can be oppressive to some and frightening to others. If you can get past that, expect cooking utensils made out of coconut wood, big terra cotta pots, celadon pottery, outdoor teak furniture, and great heavy cotton batik fabric as well as the occasional antique.

ITALY

Arezzo

PIAZZA GRANDE
First Sunday of each month
Over six hundred dealers sell a democratic mix of expensive antique furniture and religious art as well as far less expensive household goods from the '50s and '60s. (If all that sounds too rich for your blood, you'll be happy to know its also known for its reproduction ceramics and new discount merchandise.)

Florence

PIAZZO DELLE PULCE
The last Sunday of the month 9 A.M.–dusk
Pulce actually means "flea" and this is a regular gathering spot for some two hundred local vendors selling goods that can range from quasi-antique furniture to a generous selection of vintage textiles, not-so-old secondhand clothes, jewelry, bibelots, and coins. Everything is laid out on tables that snake through the street and surround a junk arcade, which

operates every day. It's great for late nineteenth- and early twentieth-century decorative arts, '60's and '70s vampish Italo mod, and oddball small items of unintentional surrealism.

If all that excitement wears you out, Fornorio on via Pulce across from the arcade is especially good for drinks and pastries.

CASCINE
Tues. 9 A.M.–1 P.M.

Though it's not exclusively flea-oriented, there are excellent secondhand clothes and textile stands within this mile-long celebration of local color. Go there for knitwear, knockoffs, weird kitchen items you can't find back home, and for pure vitality of the scene.

Rome

MERCATO DI PORTUNESE
Sun. 9 A.M.–2 P.M.

This gargantuan stretch of market along the Tiber River starts at the Porta Portunese and runs to Via Portunese. It sells almost anything imaginable, including all sorts of antiques and fake antiques. Everything from extraordinary period furniture to Art Deco classics are here. But keep your eye out for simple household chairs with good lines, small frames, architectural remnants, and especially the vintage clothes. From polyester clam diggers to leopard skin who-knows-what, the prices can be wonderfully minuscule.

MOROCCO

Home of the first bazaar and some of the most sensuous, sinuous, and luxurious collectibles imaginable. But be careful if you're in the market for antiques. Authenticity is often a problem here.

Marrakech

THE SOUK

You won't have trouble finding The Souk, but hire a guide to help you find your way back to your hotel when you're done meandering through the countless back streets and alleys that make up this celebrated marketplace. The souk is the legendary Casbah that embodied all that was once mysterious and exotic. This mysterious maze of twists and turns is packed with shop after shop of live chickens, exotic glass lanterns, three-legged brass tables, painted drinking glasses, coveted rugs, brocade pillows, semi-precious stones, elaborate tableware, embroidered leather pieces, and all kinds of collectibles that conjure up the romance of the desert.

Lisbon

ALFAMA QUARTER
Tues. and Sat. 9 A.M.–6 P.M.

This small but popular market is located behind St. Vincent's Church. It has the occasional twentieth-century glass find, as

well as traditional and quite beautiful wooden church candlesticks and all kinds of vintage linens.

RUSSIA

Shop carefully. Russian law prohibits the export of anything
more than fifty years old.

Moscow

IZMAILOVO FOREST-PARK
Eastern Moscow
Saturday and Sunday

Vast, unpredictable, and constantly evolving, Izmailovo market epitomizes the streak of anarchy that is the hallmark of
flea markets everywhere. It's a true scene.

You'll notice other Americans and Europeans trying to make
the right choices amidst an extensive selection of Russian
World War II helmets, Lenin pins and posters, icon boxes,
vintage Chinese kitsch, and Azerbaijani rugs on display.
Others will be taking a close look at more recent vintage
Gorbachev dolls, Moscow Hard Rock Cafe T-shirts, and commemorative pins. (Muscovites themselves are on the lookout for revolutionary pottery by designers like Kasimir
Malevich.)

Prices are better at the end of the weekend. If you get hungry,
you can buy caviar at bargain prices.

SOUTH AFRICA

Flea markets in South Africa are so popular—especially among wealthy Johannesburg residents—that there is a flea market on the Internet with details of locations and schedules for markets in Krugersdorp Gauteng, Phoenix Park Vanderbijlpark, and Irene Gauteng. Investigate auction houses while you're in South Africa as well. Your concierge should be able to help direct you.

Johannesburg

MARKET THEATER FLEA MARKET
Saturday A.M.

To regular and devoted enthusiasts, Market Theater Flea is a bead and batik wonderland. Wooden bowls, bowls woven from colorful telephone wire, brass bead necklaces from Cameroon, carved wooden masks, glass beads blown in Venice, beaded glass dolls, and just about everything batik under the sun. Also look for Nelson Mandela collectibles.

Note: Security is not always the best.

ROSEBANK MALL
Sunday A.M.

This flea market is held on the top level of the parking structure at the Rosebank Mall. If you don't find something special at this Sunday-only rooftop flea market, you can window shop for European goods in the mall's boutiques.

Look for wonderful carved wood, striking necklaces, and all sorts of traditional and unusual recycled twentieth-century goods.

SPAIN

Some say the wide range of goods for sale is a result of the Spanish Civil War, which made everything for sale. Spain is still sorting out the melee. In any event, late nineteenth- and early twentieth-century items are still "the new stuff" in someone's living room. There are great weekly markets and secondhand stores all over Spain.

Local Spanish flea-goers are known for their innovation. For example, they might add legs to a "cleric's suitcase" (a richly inlaid wooden box with handles used for portable saints and ritual implements) and voilà—they have a small table!

Madrid

EL RASTRO
South of the Plaza del Cascorro
Sat.–Sun. 9 A.M.–2 P.M.

Set the alarm. This is one of the best markets in Spain. It has many small courtyards filled with high-end nineteenth-century antiques from ceramics to wood carvings. If you're looking for antique brass beds, El Rastro is definitely your kind of market. And while all markets in Spain specialize in religious art, this market is especially good for religious pieces and for prints. Local shoppers also keep their eyes open for farm equipment with possibilities. For example: well-used metal and wood grain thrashers can look like primitive art, and with a piece of glass they can be transformed into a coffee table.

TAIWAN

Taipei

SHRILIN YE SHR CHANG

This is the biggest weekend flea market, and it's held in Shrilin, a suburb north of Taipei. Go during holidays like the Lantern Festival, the Dragon Festival, or one of the many other Taiwanese celebrations to get wonderful holiday collectibles.

Otherwise expect plenty of bric-a-brac, kid's toys, cosmetics, and clothing, but not much in the way of classic antiquities. However, as the concept of flea markets becomes more popular in Asia, more and more real vintage goods are starting to emerge!

THAILAND

The Thai are excited about new and modern goods and quite disdainful of older goods that they feel are kitsch. However, Chat Tu Jak offers a wonderful opportunity to see a cross-section of the Thai people amidst a riveting, thriving market scene and an enthusiastic assortment of new and older goods—with an emphasis on the new.

But be wary before you invest heavily in "antiquities" at an outdoor market; making almost anything look antique is a local specialty. The Thai government prohibits taking antiquities—such as statues of Buddha—out of Thailand. There are still many remarkable crafts produced in Thailand throughout the entire twentieth century worth trying to find, such as silver ceremonial bowls with intricate repoussé designs, black and gold lacquer ware, and evocative betel-nut boxes and containers that are beautifully crafted.

Bangkok

THE WEEKEND MARKET
at Cha Tu Jak Park off Phahonyothin Road
This market used to be held outside the Royal Palace in Bangkok, but now takes place outside the center of town. Held daily, it's mostly about socializing, but you'll also find excellent prices on a wide range of foreign antiquities, vintage painted porcelain doorknobs, amulets, celadon-colored ceramics, silver, and beautiful silks in addition to army surplus goods, American blue jeans, model airplanes, stuffed water buffalo toys, and glitter embossed pictures of the Thai monarch believed to bless a home. You'll also find real and fake gems and a lot of vintage religious statuary smuggled in from Cambodia. But if all that is not enough, check out the up and coming Thai fashion designers. They usually get their start by opening a stall at the market.

Restaurants abound around the edge of the market. Cham Long's vegetarian restaurant is particularly worth a try.

selling
made
simple

The lure of the alter-economy is not only all the adventures you can have buying, but also the remarkable learning experiences you can have when you sell. It's an Economics 101 lesson like no other.

Plus, if you're like everyone else who has indulged their passion for gathering over the years, you'll eventually be ready to pare down and sell off a few things. Whether you're doing it in the name of simplifying your life—or under the aegis of making room for the next great wave, you can become a player in the alter-economy.

The basic lesson is simple. In the alter-economy, insider logic rules: "It's only worth what someone will pay." Your task is to hunt down the person who values what you have spent time gathering. In the process, you'll gather an uncommon amount of knowledge about the all-too-human urge to acquire.

And naturally, if all goes well, selling off your goods will reward you materially. You may even experience the karmic rewards of providing pleasure for someone else. And years of buying and selling lead to interesting relationships with fellow collectors around the country and the world.

Your choices are rampant when entering the alter-economy, depending on the value of what you would like to sell. You may want to host a one-time-only garage or yard sale. You can sell to dealers at co-ops and antique malls—or you can even rent your own booth. You can set up a table at flea markets for a relatively small fee. You can call an auction house. You can rent a table at a collectibles show or consign your goods to a dealer. You can sell to a picker. Or you can float a sale on the World Wide Web.

Which one is right for you will depend on what you're selling, how valuable it is, and your comfort level with the medium. For example, if you don't use a modem, Websites are out. Or if you don't want to devote an entire day to having strangers comment on your personal possessions, yard sales and flea markets may not be viable.

But take a look at all of your options before you make a decision—and good luck!

Garage and Yard Sales

Throughout neighborhoods across the world, whether on front lawns, in alleyways, or to the side of mud huts, scores of garage and yard sales take place every weekend in the alter-economy. However, at the risk of full disclosure, hosting one can also be a big waste of time if you don't do your homework.

If you've never noticed any in your neighborhood, your first step is to see if holding a yard sale is legal. Some local governments limit the amount of sales and times of year for them. Check with your town hall or the classified ad rep of your local paper to see if there are any local ordinances you should know about before you get too far down the road.

On the other hand, your town may hold cooperative flea markets or market days that you may want to participate in because someone else is doing all the promotion and advertising. Better yet, the crowds are bigger.

Once you're psyched to host a yard, stoop, or sidewalk sale, you need to make an inventory of what you have to sell. If you're not planning to sell enough to make it look like it's worth finding a parking space, don't bother. But if you've got a lot to get rid of—especially if some of it is big (like furniture)—the classic yard sale could be your medium! Just make sure you have enough stuff displayed to make a good impression. The well-trained eye can spot a potentially good sale while traveling at the local speed limit in the indigenous form of transportation.

And nobody is going to slam on the brakes for an outdated Mr. Coffee, a stained pot holder, and the remnants of your Mr. Potato Head kit that you've spread out on a blanket. So think about what would make you stop. In fact, drive by a few sales before you plan yours. Get a sense for what makes some sales look interesting and others look like duds. If you think you're not going to be able to create the necessary impact with your own grouping of items get some friends, neighbors, or family members to contribute.

Think of your conglomerate presentation as the difference between a mom and pop store and the obvious appeal of a monster Superstore. Plus, if your neighbors host a sale at the same time you do, it will create more excitement and you will lessen the chance of annoying the people you live next to. And a tent might be a nice touch.

Don't overlook timing either. In most areas, the spring and fall are your best periods for a successful garage or yard sale. These are the seasons people are most inspired to clean out their cluttered homes, make a new decorating statement, or move to another place in which case they'll need "things." Plus, if summer is too hot, people get lazy and aren't as motivated to get out of their air-conditioned cars. Exceptions are tourist areas, where year-round sales will draw an audience.

Once you've got your inventory list and a date, it's not that hard to produce a show stopper. Garage and yard sales are now so popular that many stationery and party supply stores stock preprinted signs and banners for you to promote your big event. You can post these along the bigger highways near the entrance streets. Tack up an announcement on local community bulletin boards in supermarkets or churches. Yard sale fanatics keep as close an eye on these informal media as they do on the classified section.

But for the best results, you'll need an ad. Check the rates and deadlines in advance for daily, weekly, and "shopper" newspapers. See which one runs the most yard sale classifieds—that's the one that probably pulls in the most shoppers. Run your ad on Thursday and through the weekend. (In many areas, Thursday has become the day of choice for garage and yard sale fanatics to plan their weekend route.)

A good headline will differentiate your ad, and since an advertising agency is not likely to take you on pro bono, this is your opportunity to write the kind of catchy headline you take for granted in your daily life.

What's catchy? Good question. If you're selling a high-interest item like furniture, sporting goods, or office equipment, make sure it's prominent in the headline—that's what translates to "catchy" in the alter-economy. Remember you want to attract people who are looking for what you have to sell, so if you've got it, flaunt it. And be sure to write your address and any important directions in language that will aid a map-impaired reader. Your address, after all, is your second-most important statement.

Your other key promotional activity is to prepare signs. This is your opportunity to show off your design skills, or you might want to buy a preprinted version from a stationery store. Take down your signs after the event or an irritated neighbor might follow the directions and read you the riot act.

With an ad placed two to three weeks ahead, now is the time to document your offerings. Set up space in your garage, shed, or ballroom and start tagging items. Include the asking price and if you know the make, model, year or any other information that will assist in selling the item. You may need to do some homework in establishing prices. Stop by local flea markets, junk stores, antique malls, and attend a few other local yard sales so you can see what they are asking—and what they are actually getting. You don't want to give away your mint condition Ring-Ding juice glass set for 50 cents to a dealer who is planning to mark it up to $50.

Believe it or not many of the people who show up to enticing sounding garage sales are pickers and collectors. Be ready to bargain with a knowledgeable group. But once you decide on your minimum price, stick to it. You might feel better donating an item to a worthy charity than selling it for too little.

With everything priced, tagged, and a written power of attorney for anyone else's items to be included in the sale, you are ready to think about how to arrange everything.

Display techniques help. Simple things like putting flowers on a table with tablewares can help make a winning impression. So can clustering similar things on a table or neatly on the floor. You may also want to organize a special $1 table or a children's toy's section.

It should go without saying that cleanliness is a very good thing in people as well as products. Run glasses through the dishwasher if they're dusty. Ditto plates. Dust off those appliances and lamp shades, also keep an extension cord handy to show that electrical items actually work.

You may even want to take advantage of an advertising research tip: Items on the right will attract the eye first. Ergo, placing your most desirable, most profitable items on the right side should help move them faster.

Then set your alarm. Keep in mind that early birds will arrive no matter what time you set for your sale. Be prepared. Have someone else handle the cash, this will leave you free to "work the crowd," negotiate, and keep your eye on things. Just make sure to have change on hand. We do not recommend taking checks, but if you know the person or where to find them, you might consider it.

Good luck, and remember you do not have to report the income to the IRS unless you get more for an item than you originally paid for it. (It's yet another reason for the growth of the alter-economy!)

Selling on Consignment

If you've only got a few things you think are valuable to sell, consider consignment. Your choices in selling this way include auction houses, antique malls, co-ops, pawn shops, and specialty collectable retailers.

Selling on consignment simply means that you, for a fee, contract with a person or a company to sell your things on your behalf. If you have items of considerable value or if you are trying to reach a customer who is used to buying in this manner, it makes a lot of sense. Consignment selling is also an alternative for anyone who simply doesn't have the time or the interest in personally meeting with potential buyers and would feel more comfortable having a professional negotiate for them.

The way it works is simple. You agree to a specific length of time—usually two or three months—but it could be longer. If the object is relatively new (like clothing) the dealer will ask you what you paid for it, and then tell you what it might sell for in the shop. Of that price, consignment clothing dealers will sometimes keep as much as 60 percent of the asking price. In other words, if you are selling something you paid $100 dollars for and the shop owner estimates it can be resold for $40, you will get $16. Or you could have something you paid $2 for twenty years ago that is now worth $50 and you would get $20. The owner or dealer will write you a receipt with the specific terms of the arrangement. If the object doesn't sell, you get it back. It pays to keep an eye on the item. Not all shop owners or their staff are great book keepers. They will forget to call you to say a sale has been made or ask you to come by and pick up your piece because the agreed upon time limit has elapsed.

Auction Houses

If you have something reasonably valuable to sell, consider an auction house. Auction houses such as Christie's or Sotheby's have become household names for helping the well-to-do sell off excess goods. But these big guns are only the tip of the iceberg. In most cities, you have a choice of auction houses. To find them, look in your phone book, ask around, or contact some of the ones we've listed.

If you do decide to use an auction house, choose one based on location, specialty, reputation, terms, etc. Auction houses can be excellent places to find suitable buyers, but they can't guarantee that you'll get the price you are looking for. You can decrease your risk by asking the auction house to place a minimum (known as a reserve) on the item, which tends to be effective on higher priced merchandise.

"Be Here with Me at $10,000"

Here is a brief listing of auction houses that illustrates just how specialized they can be:

A.N. ABELL AUCTION COMPANY
2613 Yates Avenue
Commerce, CA 90040
☎ (213) 734-4151
This is one of the largest estate auction houses in Los Angeles, and it's especially big with the decorator and dealer set.

AMERICA WEST ARCHIVES

P.O. Box 100

Cedar City, UT 84721

☎ (801) 586-9497

America West holds auctions six times per year featuring early
Western ephemera, autographs, documents, letters, photographs,
and other general paper. Strictly mail bids. Call for a catalog.

ANDERSON AUCTION

P.O. Box 644

Troy, OH 45373

☎ (513) 339-0850

Americana from folk art to furniture is their specialty.

F.O. BAILEY & CO.

141 Middle Street

Portland, ME 04101

☎ (207) 774-1479

Once a month they have a specialized auction; call for the
schedule. They also have a retail store with antiques, jewelry,
lamps, and other 1960s collectibles.

JAMES R. BAKKER, INC.

236 Newbury Street

Boston, MA 02116

☎ (617) 262-8020

Their auctions feature paintings, prints, and sculpture of the
nineteenth and twentieth centuries, with an emphasis on
contemporary America.

BUTTERFIELD & BUTTERFIELD

7601 Sunset Boulevard

Los Angeles, CA 90046

☎ (213) 850-7500

This is a major auction house with multiple locations. Each features estate sales, twentieth-century photography, jewelry, furniture, and special events.

CHRISTIE'S
502 Park Avenue
New York, NY 10022
☎ (212) 546-1000

One of the major auction houses in the world. Christie's offers representation worldwide. They offer a multitude of specialty auctions, estate sales, and educational programs. Call for more information or check them out on the Web at http://www.christies.com

CINCINNATI ART GALLERIES
635 Main Street
Cincinnati, OH 45202
☎ (513) 381-2128

A live auction is held once a year for ceramics and American art pottery. A catalog is available.

RUSS COCHRAN'S COMIC ART AUCTIONS
P.O. Box 469
West Plains, MO 65775
☎ (417) 256-2224

Comic strip art is their specialty. You can bid via phone and mail auctions as well as quarterly public auctions. Call for a catalog.

WILLIAM DOYLE GALLERIES
175 E. 87th Street
New York, NY 10128
☎ (212) 427-2730

Handles estate sales on consignment, general antiques, and well-made furnishings like overstuffed chairs and furniture.

FINE WINE AUCTIONS
535 Madison Avenue
New York, NY 10022
☎ (212) 307-4200
Their specialty is California wines—however, they also handle
German and Italian wines, Bordeaux, and ports.

FRANK'S ANTIQUES
P.O. Box 516
Hilliard, FL 32046
☎ (904) 845-2870
If you want to bid on or sell advertising and tobacco collectibles,
this is the auction house to call.

LYNN GEYER'S ADVERTISING AUCTIONS
300 Trail Ridge
Silver City, NM 88061
☎ (505) 538-2341
Advertising ephemera is their mainstay.

GLASS-WORKS AUCTIONS
P.O. Box 187
East Greenville, PA 18041
☎ (215) 679-5849
No surprise here. Glass-Works specializes in glass and
bottles.

GREENBERG AUCTIONS
7566 Main Street
Sykesville, MD 21784
☎ (410) 795-7447
Train sets and other collectible toys are their specialty. They
conduct live auctions and mail/phone bids three to four times per
year. Call for their schedule and catalog.

GENE HARRIS ANTIQUE AUCTION CENTER
203 S. 18th Avenue
Marshalltown, IA 50158
☎ (515) 752-0600
The Center specializes in turn-of-the-century antiques. They hold
auctions for clocks, toys, art glass, and other categories. (Their live
auctions are held once a week. Call for a schedule and catalog.)

HESSE GALLERIES
20 Main Street
Otego, NY 13825
☎ (607) 988-6322
Weekly auctions of American fine art and antiques. (They also
hold household consignment auctions mid-week.)

ILLUSTRATION HOUSE
96 Spring St.
New York, NY 10012
☎ (212) 966-9444
They handle original artwork done for reproduction circa
1880–1960. (If reprinted on a magazine cover, they handle original
artwork only.)

Illustration House conducts auctions annually, and they also
handle consignment for private buyers.

IVY & MADER PHILATELIC AUCTIONS INC.
32 E. 57th Street
New York, NY 10022
☎ (212) 486-1222 or (800) 782-6771
Ivy & Mader deals exclusively in collector stamps. Along with a
sister company, Greg Manning in New Jersey, they are the largest
stamp auction house in the country. Auctions are held four times a
year.

LAMBERTVILLE ANTIQUE AND AUCTION CENTER
333 North Main Street
Lambertville, NJ 08530
☎ (609) 397-9374
These monthly auctions focus on twentieth-century decorative arts, Mission oak furniture, and Art Deco to modern furniture. They also hold an absentee pottery auction twice a year.

HOWARD LOWERY
3810 West Magnolia Boulevard
Burbank, CA 91505
☎ (818) 972-9080
Animation art is their specialty.

GREG MANNING AUCTIONS, INC.
775 Passaic Avenue
West Caldwell, NJ 07006
☎ (201) 882-0004
Sister company to Ivy & Mader in New York City. They exclusively auction stamps four times a year.

DAN MAY & ASSOCIATES
4110 N. Scottsdale Road
Scottsdale, AZ 85251
☎ (602) 941-4200
They auction once a year in October. American nineteenth- and twentieth-century paintings and sculpture are the house specialty.

METROPOLITAN ARTS AND ANTIQUES PAVILION
110 W. 19th St.
New York, NY 10011
☎ (212) 463-0200
Handles works on paper and autographed books; they also have specialized auctions and antique fairs.

NEW ORLEANS AUCTION GALLERIES, INC.

801 Magazine Street
New Orleans, LA 70130
☎ (504) 566-1849

Eight auctions per year! Their specialty is the decorative arts.

PHILLIPS NEW YORK

406 E. 79th Street
New York, NY 10021
☎ (212) 570-4830

This firm auctions modern and antique jewelry, watches, Judaica books and art, golf memorabilia, toys and collectibles, chess sets and related items, natural history, art, fine wines, and American paintings and prints.

POSTER AUCTIONS INTERNATIONAL, INC.

601 W. 26th Street
New York, NY 10001
☎ (212) 787-4000

They specialize in vintage posters of the nineteenth and twentieth centuries. Call for their catalog and auction schedule if you're buying or selling.

DAVID RAGO AUCTIONS, INC.

17 South Main Street
Lambertville, NJ 08530
☎ (609) 397-9374

Art pottery and Arts and Crafts movement, twentieth-century decorative modern, and general lines all appear on their auction block. Live auctions are scheduled once a month, with phone and mail bids accepted as well. You can call for their catalog.

RED BARON'S ANTIQUES

6450 Roswell Road
Atlanta, GA 30328

☎ (404) 252-3770

This unusual auction house features large and unusual architectural antiques.

L.H. SELMAN LTD.

761 Chestnut Street

Santa Cruz, CA 95060

☎ (408) 427-1177

Crystal paperweights only! Auctions held twice a year.

SOTHEBY'S

1334 York Avenue

New York, NY 10021

☎ (212) 606-7000

Sotheby's provides a broad range of ancillary services which are valuable to collectors. They have offices across the world and provide excellent educational services. Check them out on the Web at http://www.sothebys.com

SPORTING ANTIQUITIES

47 Leonard Road

Melrose, MA 02176

☎ (617) 662-6588

Not surprisingly Sporting Antiquities auctions off golf, tennis, and other sporting collectibles. Their mail, phone, and live auction is held once a year. A catalog is available.

SUPERIOR STAMP & COIN

9478 W. Olympic Boulevard

Beverly Hills, CA 90212

☎ (310) 203-9855

Not surprisingly, given their name, Superior handles stamps and coins. They also handle sports memorabilia and other collectibles through auctions and catalogs.

Additional Auction Houses can be found in your local Yellow Pages, through local antique guides, and by asking dealers at flea markets and stores. Other more complete listings of auction houses can be purchased at most book stores.

As the seller, or consignee, you might have to wait a fair amount of time for your items to be placed on the block. This is because in most major cities auction houses will cluster sales of similar items at the same time. For example, tapestries might go on sale only in February in Chicago or May in New York. By clustering sales, auction houses cooperate to encourage buyers to travel and participate in many sales over a period of several days.

Look for auction houses and auctioneers who understand your particular category; they will have a much better understanding of how to price and describe the items to the buying audience. The larger the auction house the more likely they are to have many different departments, which will be worthwhile if you want to sell a variety of items at one time. If you have a specific collection, such as Lionel Trains, you may want to search out a specialty house.

Terms differ at auction houses so be sure to interview a few candidates before making a decision. Commissions can vary from 5–25 percent and services can include catalogs, advertising, pickup, and delivery. Ask a million questions, and read the contract—carefully!

Antique Malls, Co-Ops, and Consignment Stores

Antique malls, co-ops, and consignment stores are fast becoming the most desirable and ubiquitous arenas for the sale of antiques and collectibles. These establishments come in all forms, from private basements in Connecticut to impersonal Los Angeles strip malls. Many cities now have main streets that were vacant for many years but are now thriving, as entrepreneurs open eclectic antique/junk stores and co-op-type centers.

These venues come in all sizes, from sprawling antique malls to small, discriminating boutiques, and offer you the unique opportunity to find a reputable dealer that specializes in your particular category. Some might buy your goods outright. Others, like antique mall dealers, might buy from you on consignment. And if you develop a good relationship with a few proprietors, then you will have steady access to a marketplace as well as the opportunity to buy specifically to fuel this channel. In short, you could become a picker or a dealer.

The biggest differences among antique malls, co-ops, and consignment stores is in their operating structure. Antique malls are simply facilities that house multiple dealers. Many of these facilities are retrofitted commercial properties, farmhouses, or custom buildings. These malls function as a grouping of individual dealers or as a coop situation, where one outlet may be run by a combination of dealers.

If you decide to leave your goods with a consignment store or an antique mall, the procedures and the degree of profitability can vary a lot. We advise you to check into the rental, commissions, and other financial obligations carefully. Don't leave a valuable possession with the first dealer you speak to. Bring a photograph and show it to a few different dealers or shop owners to compare their offers.

Yet if you find yourself successful in selling via these outlets and you are buying more and more items to sell, you may want to set up shop yourself. Or at least rent a space at an antique mall. The more established malls and co-ops have waiting lists for people who want to have a booth of their own, and it may take some time for you to find the situation that is right for you. During this period it might be wise to build your inventory and make alliances with other dealers that you're not in competition with so you can buy for each other. Nobody ever said the alter-economy isn't complicated.

Don't jump into anything without really thinking through issues of markup versus rent. Estimate how much you would have to sell a month—even in slow months—to cover your rent. It's harder than you might think, since you'll also need money to keep buying new stock.

Fees charged by dealers in malls, co-ops, and consignment stores to display, advertise, and sell your things vary. Not all of these dealers accept merchandise on consignment and those that do can charge 20–35 percent for the service. So venture carefully. The benefit to you of course is that you don't have to be there, pay rent, or set up shop. Most dealers will be more responsive if you become a consistent source of quality merchandise and help keep their shop well stocked. As with any other business arrangement, make sure to write down and have both parties sign the accepted terms. These terms will include pricing, acceptable discounting, payments, etc.

You can find listings in the Yellow Pages under the "consignment store," "antique mall," and "collectibles" sections. Local newspapers are also a good source for finding your perfect dealer-partner.

Flea Markets

Flea markets are often the first venue that a typical collector thinks about when trying to decide where and how to get into the selling game. One of the advantages of a good flea market is the sheer variety of the kinds of markets that exist. Some are no more than drive-in movie theaters that rent parking lot space on the weekends to anybody with something to sell. Some are held in parking lots. Others are in cavernous buildings with established dealers who return to the same space every weekend.

If you think a particular flea market is right for what you would like to sell, one option is to simply approach a dealer whose merchandise indicates an appreciation for your category and find out if he or she is interested in buying from you.

If you are thinking of actually setting up a table or a blanket, take the time to visit the grouping of markets that are in your territory. If you go much further afield, you could start having to factor in hotel and travel expenses. So explore markets that are no more than a day trip, and compare the size of the crowds and what items are most popular.

You will also want to find out how much you'll have to pay the management company per day to set up shop. Call the owner, manager, or leasing agent and find out about the terms and conditions or stop by the office (which is almost always on the property) and pick up their rate sheet. The terms vary but are mostly based on a flat daily fee. Daily fees can range from $5 to more than $20.

By studying what kinds of things are selling and how much they are selling for you'll be able to determine what you can comfortably charge. Research is easy: dealers love to talk. Especially if you are not a potential competitor. Asking casual questions can help you get the inside scoop. More importantly, you can make a rough guess as to whether or not you'll be able to charge a price that will cover the cost of renting a table and let you make a profit that would be sufficient for setting up at the crack of dawn, packing and unpacking, and sitting in the sun for hours—or in a damp parking garage—especially if you only sell a few things.

Think big. The players and the landscape are changing all the time. Check out the information provided in the next chapter on the World Wide Web and you'll see that your selling options are widening considerably.

What's It Really Worth?

Many auction houses will appraise your collections or individual items, but if you want more information on appraisers, contact one of the organizations below:

Appraisal Organizations

AMERICAN SOCIETY OF APPRAISERS
P.O. Box 17265
Washington, DC 20041
☎ (703) 620-3838

ANTIQUE APPRAISAL ASSOCIATION OF AMERICA
11361 Garden Grove Boulevard
Garden Grove, CA 92643
☎ (714) 530-7090

INTERNATIONAL SOCIETY OF APPRAISERS
P.O. Box 726
Hoffman Estates, IL 60195
☎ (708) 882-0706

Tag Sales

Occasionally you may want to sell off almost everything and the value of the possessions you want to sell doesn't lead you to believe that an auction house would be interested in handling the event for you.

Maybe you inherited your pack rat aunt's house and all of her things. Maybe you're moving to Budapest to open a coffee house and want to travel light. Or possibly, you're paring down to become a Buddhist monk.

All kinds of for-instance situations can compel you to hold a tag sale, where almost everything that isn't nailed down is for sale. Buyers are invited to wander around the house and poke around at will.

It's a big job to price so many possessions, tag everything, keep an inventory list, and negotiate with complete strangers for things that may have great sentimental value to you. You'll find yourself remembering when you bought something, how much you paid for it, and replaying favorite memories.

Many people frequently hire professionals to take care of everything. These experts are called tag sale consultants. Tag sale consultants do most of the negotiating—and they work on commission, so the more money you make, the more money they make.

Usually, they have hands-on experience in affixing value to just about anything. Before you choose one, go to a few tag sales that you see advertised in the classifieds. You'll not only meet these consultants, but you'll probably have an immediate sense of which one you would want to have help you sell off your worldly goods for a profit.

"How Much Is It?"

No matter where you decide to sell, the pricing issue will always be present. The following tips may help:

☆ When you're deciding what price to charge for something, keep in mind that most people will ask for a better deal. It's just the way things are. Think of it as fun. However, if you have something valuable, ask someone who knows the category for advice. If it appears that you are in for a windfall, don't be greedy; after all, you have to find someone to actually buy the item first.

♣ You can ask more for something that's clean and in good repair. If you do not have to go to much trouble to do minor repairs, i.e. rewire a lamp, do them.

✳ When you're selling, always evaluate the situation; try to spot the pro from the novice who has a true passion for the piece. Very often someone who wants the item for themselves will pay more than a dealer who is looking to turn it around for a profit.

✱ Hard-selling techniques usually backfire, especially if you're thinking of becoming a dealer—and not just a dealer for a day. If you want longevity, you have to sell through knowledge and subtleties. Respect your customers' space. Don't crowd them. A friendly acknowledgment when they enter your area works until the customer indicates they would like your help. (Saying "Good-bye" is also a good strategy.)

✳ The single most important rule to remember is that things don't talk, you have to do it for them. The more you know about what you're selling, the more natural this will be. An enthusiastic dealer who values what he has to sell can usually communicate this to a customer and earn their respect. So keep in mind the most valuable asset in both buying and selling is knowledge. This includes knowledge in the categories of objects you are dealing with as well as knowledge of "the art of the deal."

☆ People want to hear all about the details of what they are buying. So even if all you know is how you came across an item, tell the story. But better yet, tell them how old it is, what it's made of, and why it's special. Don't make things up, though.

net
value
websites

10

Much like Baby Huey, alter-economy Websites are still in their evolutionary infancy, but their sophistication is growing exponentially. The possibilities range from little more than decorative home pages to on-line auctions offering some remarkable bargains. Some are floated by visitors bureaus, some by tour guides, and some by shop proprietors. Some are informational, some are idiosyncratic, and some are well-established bidding sites for serious collectors.

There are even a surprising number of Websites to help you learn more about international markets. You can find out the latest trends in South African flea markets, get directions to relatively small Canadian markets, or details on a gay and lesbian flea market tour of Paris.

In short, you can wheel and deal for just about anything on the World Wide Web at any time of the day or night. And while these virtual flea markets and auctions can't replace touching and feeling or obscure roadside adventures, they can be an incredible resource for both buyers and sellers. (In this chapter we will focus on buying—however most on-line dealers and resources also allow sellers to advertise or link-up in some way.)

Start Here

In order to browse World Wide Web (WWW) site markets you'll need a computer and a modem. If you're just now buying a modem make sure to get at least a 28.8 speed modem. (The artistic complexity of many Websites will be glacially slow at a lesser speed.)

Besides a modem, you'll also need an on-line account. You have many choices here: select one of the leading on-line services such as America Online (AOL), Prodigy, or CompuServe, or pay a monthly fee to an Internet provider and use Netscape or Microsoft Explorer as a browser. In the interest of speed we recommend using an Internet provider for direct access to the Web.

An on-line account lets you set up an e-mail address, which allows you to send and receive mail over the Internet. (Your e-mail address is your connection to fellow "junkers" around the world.) You can find out about dealers, collectors, associations, magazines, books, events, antiques, etc., through home pages on the WWW or through Internet newsgroups called Usenet. Usenet is the global distribution system of newsgroups. People from all over the world discuss everything imaginable, including collectibles.

Once you're armed with a computer, a modem, and an on-line account, go surfing on the World Wide Web. When you are on the Web, you may want to find the "bookmark" function on the browser and use it whenever you come across a site that you want to visit frequently. (You can also set up folders in which you can store Web addresses for future reference.)

The etiquette is fairly standard. Most auction Websites follow the policy that you take an item "as is, where is." Most of them also let you return it after a five to seven day inspection period. But before you bid always ask what the policy is for the specific site. And remember that as a buyer you are also responsible for paying taxes, shipping, and insurance. Plus, most sites have minimum bids. And most notify bidders by e-mail if their bid was accepted or bettered.

One more word to the wise. Some services charge the seller fees of up to 10 percent—but some charge the buyer. (Ask *before* you bid, not after!)

A good place to start exploring the electronic alter-economy is with one of the major search engines. They are invaluable in helping you search for your topic of interest among thousands of sites. To use these search engines, simply type in general words like: "antiques and collectibles," "flea markets," or specific categories like "Russel Wright silverware" and you are bound to find more listings than there are dealers at Brimfield.

And at the risk of noting the obvious, the more time you spend in investigative surfing, the more rewards you will find.

The following are a few major search engine sites of note and more are coming on-line all the time. Services such as Dejanews will put you directly in touch with people with similar interests and no doubt turn you on to more interesting sites.

YAHOO
http://www.yahoo.com
LYCOS
http://www.lycos.com
ALTAVISTA
http://www.altavista.com
EXCITE
http://www.excite.com
DEJANEWS
http://www.dejanews.com
INFOSEEK
http://www.infoseek.com

Alter-Markets, Auction Sites, & Collector Chat Rooms

The listings below are just a taste of what's out there. Every one of these Websites is remarkably like the real thing, and once you get going it will be hard not to keep going back.

After you've started with some of the sites listed below, you'll be able to spread your wings and keep your ear to the buzz. New sites appear every day. Plus, you'll be making new friends in unexpected places along the way.

ABILENE ANTIQUE SHOPS AND FLEA MARKETS
http://www.abilene.com/visitors/antique.html
The Abilene, Texas, Visitors Bureau floats this definitive listing of their local flea markets and antique shops.

AMERICAN MODERN
http://www.derby.k12.ks.us/~rwright/wright.html
Visit this site on a regular basis if you love Russel Wright pottery.

ANTIQUES AND COLLECTIBLES GUIDE
http://tias.com/amdir/info.html
If you're planning to travel internationally, or you're looking for a Turkish damascene sword, start at this Website. It lists events around the world, has a worldwide shop locator, and lists specialties by categories.

ANTIQUES ON-LINE
http://www.auctions-on-line.com
Sellers buy space on this site to let you know they are out there. So while you can't buy directly from this site, you'll be able to make connections with some dealers.

ANTIQUE TRAILS
http://netnow.micron.net/trails~index.html
If you're a fan of Northwestern antiques, collectibles, and contemporary wares, then happy trails are ahead. Auctions at this site include Indian blankets, pottery, and jewelry.

ANTKONLINE SERVICES, INC.
http://suba.com/ANTKonLINE/
This on-line antique mall is quite the electronic shopping destination for twentieth-century artifacts. Check out the links.

A–Z ANTIQUE & COLLECTIBLE DIRECTORY
http://www.curioscape.com
An index of over 1,500 Websites. Promotes the WWW as a tool for antiquing and collecting.

CHRISTIE'S AUCTIONEERS
http://www.christies.com

One of the most famous worldwide auction houses is also on the Web. Click to preview a variety of departments, scheduled auctions, catalogs, and contacts.

CLASSIC RADIO GALLERY
http://members.aol.com/djadamson/arp.html

You'll want to tune in immediately—if you collect radios.

FABERGE TOUR OF FLEA MARKETS
http://faberge.com/places/paris/paris/htm

Looking for a scenic, essentially non-verbal break? This purely photogenic tour of chic collectibles from vintage silver champagne buckets to early scrolled ironwork is quite restful if nothing else.

GAY AND LESBIAN TOURS OF PARIS FLEA MARKETS
http://www.cnct.com/home/lifestyl/parismkt.html

This is a specialized Website put together by the guides themselves describing the tour they sell to the Porte de Montreuil Market, the Market at Porte de Vanves, and the Porte de Cligancourt. This site includes information on the Paris Gay Pride Parade and after-parade parties.

HAWAII COLLECTIBLES IN PARADISE
http://www.ahoha.com/~shakacat/index.html

There are no ocean breezes at this tropical Website, but you'll find plenty of salt shakers, hula girls, and milkcaps.

INDEX OF EPHEMERA, COLLECTIBLES & NOSTALGIA WEB SITES
http://serve.com/ephemera/collectibles/index.html

This site will link you up to specialized associations, clubs, and dealers as well as give you the inside skinny on interesting markets and sites worth visiting.

INTERNET ANTIQUE SHOP
http://www.tias.com
This one is a must visit. One of the most comprehensive antique and collectible sites currently on the Internet. Make sure to look at the discussion groups under "cool stuff."

INTERNET AUCTION LIST
http://www.usaweb.com/auction.html
Need a listing of hundreds of live auction sites and a breakdown of schedules broken down by category? Start here.

LEARN ABOUT ANTIQUES AND COLLECTIBLES
http://willow.internet-connections.net/web/antiques/
This is a useful resource for the novice collector on many of the key aspects of buying. It gives examples and images of common collectibles and has a surprisingly varied scope.

MERCATORS WORLD
http://mercatormag.com
See the world without getting lost. This magazine-based Website features collectible maps.

MUNICH FLEA MARKETS
http://www.munichfound.de/issues/1996/6/articles/
　WhatsUp/Flea.html
Need phone numbers and addresses of flea and collector's markets in Munich? Click here. Better yet, this site is cross-referenced by stamps, books, toys, and antiques so you don't have to waste a minute at the wrong booth.

NET COLLECTIBLES
http://www.netcollectibles.com
This on-line mall is quite the coffee klatch. It's dedicated to bringing buyers and sellers together. A chat room is available to compare notes and it also has a search function. With it, you can browse over fifty dealers with their own pages.

NETIS AUCTIONS ON THE WEB
http://www.netis.com
Netis provides auction information such as dates and places. Plus, it functions as a search engine for your specific area of interest. Register via e-mail to receive updates on current auctions. Use their extensive list of links to find out about a host of other related sites.

NEW YORK CITY GUIDE TO THRIFT SHOPS
AND FLEA MARKETS
http://www.allny.com/thrift.html#fm
This definitive Website is a rare find. It's an in-depth resource guide for anyone living in or visiting any borough in New York City. It gives you a helpful review of every flea market, thrift shop, secondhand store, damaged goods store, and consignment shop in Manhattan, Queens, Brooklyn, the Bronx, and Staten Island—complete with addresses and phone numbers.

NUMISMATISTS ONLINE
http://www.numismatists.com
Bid for early coins and medals from ancient times, Mexico, and Colonial America at this fascinating and quite competitive on-line auction.

OHIO FLEA MARKETS
http://www.bargain-mall.com/Oh.html
Nothing fancy. It does, however, have directions, phone numbers, and dates for markets in Amherst, Ashtabula, Fremont, Hartville, and Springfield.

ONSALE AUCTION HOUSE
http://www.onsale.com
One of the first transaction sites on the Web. These days it has become far more commercial. Have a credit card ready, submit

your bid on a wide variety of collectibles and memorabilia, then check your e-mail to see if it's all yours.

OPEN AIR MARKETS
http://www.openair.org

If you think about it, this site is quite the global village wonder. It's an extensive guide to street markets, flea markets, and farmers' markets around the world. It will help you find markets and links to markets on every continent.

PARISCOPE
http://pariscope.fr

The most comprehensive listing of flea markets in and around Paris. Print out the maps and times before you leave home. Au revoir.

PASTIMES ANTIQUES AND COLLECTIBLES
http://pastimes.com

This is an on-line catalog that will also do custom searches for you. They also buy collections, especially Bakelite, photography, and political memorabilia.

PHILATELISTS ONLINE
http://www.philatelists.com

If you're a stamp collector, then you've probably already discovered this auction site. The rules here are simple. The highest bidder doesn't have to pay more than five percent more than the second highest bidder. The site also holds mock auctions, so first-time bidders can practice bidding!

PORT ELIZABETH, SOUTH AFRICA
http://196.3.224.120/tourism/atflea.htm

This home page for the attractions of Port Elizabeth includes directions to the local flea markets and local updates like a description of the first Sunday of the month craft fair held at St. George's Park.

SAMMY'S SOHO ANTIQUE STORE
http://www.telenet.net/commercial/sammys
The hip SoHo store can also be reached on the net, although the range of goods tends to be on the higher end. Still, you never know what will be pictured in this catalog-format site.

SOTHEBY'S AUCTIONEERS
http://www.sothebys.com
This distinguished auction house site is always worth a visit, especially their "Collectors Corner." It's a great place to learn about specific areas as well as to find out about links to newsgroups.

SOUTH AFRICAN CALENDAR OF EVENTS
http://www.africa.com/satour
Need addresses and dates for markets in Irene, Pretoria, Vanderbijlpark, Krugersdorp, and the Botanical Institute of Pretoria? Then this is the site for you.

20TH CENTURY ANTIQUES AND COLLECTIBLES STORE
http://www.koan.com/~pjones
The name of the store tells it all quite succinctly. Browse its electronic aisles for pottery, furniture, lighting, black Americana, golf collectibles, etc.

VIRTUAL FLEA MARKET
http://www.bright.net/~sschuler/flea.html
The Virtual Flea Market lists and sells a range of general collectibles. Like any market it may—or may not—be for you on any given day. Luckily, the stock is always changing.

A Background Bite

The Internet is a structurally decentralized system that sends packets of electronic information along whatever route is open, to be reassembled at their destination. Thanks to a graphical user interface known as Mosaic, which was developed at Northwestern University in early 1993 and later evolved into Netscape, Internet access has allowed for general accessibility, much socializing, and at-home junking.

In fact, the Internet is such an innately social medium you can have more conversations than you might ever have at an actual market, although they won't be quite as random. Plus, the chance to spot something unexpected from the corner of your eye is also lower since the act of scanning images into their computers causes Website dealers to do a little editing. On the other hand, the Web lets you look at chairs, stamps, and finds from exotic markets or the other side of the country and the planet. Rain or shine. Best of all, you can correspond with other collectors once you've met by e-mail or in chat rooms.

So while they rarely replace the adrenaline kick of the real thing—they sure can supplement it.

All things are metaphor.
—Goethe

Sheila Zubrod currently lives in New York City, where she frequents the 26th Street Flea Market on a regular basis. As a child she collected empty milk cartons, dolls, and the complete adventures of the Bobbsey Twins, Nancy Drew, and the Hardy Boys. Her current collection encompasses contact lens solutions, eighteen-inch lengths of barbed wire, and Moroccan-influenced dinnerware. She believes flea markets are one of the great privileges of living at the end of the twentieth century.

David Stern is a partner with the prominent graphic design firm Maddocks and Company. He has furthered his love of design by indulging in the hunt for things with aesthetic and cultural significance. He is not a compulsive collector but rather is an adventurous browser with an eye for eclectic objects, art, and furnishings. David currently resides with his wife in Venice Beach, California.